# Live to

# Win!

---

**5 Essentials for**

**Your Victory and Success**

---

Evangeline Colbert

D1089214

Original Image credits: Hammer by Khunaspix | Umbrella by Idea Go | FreeDigital Photos

Cover Design by Veraline Stover
Cover Photography by Haz Sunsets Photography

# PRAISE FOR *LIVE TO WIN!*

*Live to Win* is a powerful tool that needs to be in the hands of everyone looking to experience victory in *any* area of life. Evangeline has given us powerful strategies that are packed with the wisdom of God. She outlines five essential principles that become blueprints and pathways leading to successful living. These are all based on the promises of God and they help the reader easily transform the way they live.

*~Dr. Frederick R. Browning,* Senior Pastor of SonRise Faith Community Center and Author of *Dream Your Destiny*

## MY PRAYER FOR YOU

I pray that every day, especially in days of trouble and distress, you'll remember the Lord loves you and is *with* you. May He give you wisdom and send you aid to support, refresh, and strengthen you.

May He grant your heart's desire and fulfill all your plans, giving you a life of good success. May He show you how to rise and stand firm. I pray you live each day believing in His love for you; believing in His power to bring you through anything and everything as a victor.

May God help you to see that you are already a winner in Christ.

I pray that what is contained within the pages of this book will produce a powerful effect on you. As you read it, may you see the truth in its message and, as you apply that truth, may it set you free to "Live to Win". May you be empowered to proclaim Jesus' words from Luke 4:19— that *this* is a season of God's favor in your life.

May this book serve you so that you become all you were born to be—a champion!

AMEN.

~Evangeline

# TABLE OF CONTENTS

# INTRODUCTION

*Rise from the dust.*
*Sit in a place of honor.*
Isaiah 52:2 NLT

The eleventh commandment should be, "Thou shall not sweat."

I know "sweatless" success doesn't seem very practical. And for most of us, it's hard to step aside and let someone else take on what we see as our work or our battle. But instead of working up a sweat to force good things to happen in your life, God wants you to rest in Him and allow Him to do the heavy lifting. He wants you to rise from your dusty place of self-effort and sit in a place of honor where you enjoy His favor in every aspect of your life. He wants you seated in the position of honor that Jesus' sacrifice made possible for you.

God wants you to rest while He does the work of battle against the enemy of your success. Allow God's grace—His unearned, unmerited, and "sweatless" favor—to work on your behalf. Let the ultimate Victor show you *how to stop being a victim of your circumstances.* He wants to show you how to let go, enjoy His flow, and **live to win**.

> *Get away with Me and you'll recover your life. I'll*
> *show you how to take a real rest. Walk with Me and*

*work with me—watch how I do it. Learn the unforced rhythms of grace. I won't lay anything heavy or ill-fitting on you. Keep company with Me and you'll learn to live freely and lightly.* Matthew 11: 29-30 MSG

Let Go. Enjoy His Flow. **Live to Win.**

Everyone wants to live life with victory, purpose and hope. We all look for ways to rise above adversity and live a lifestyle that is full of peace, success, and wholeness. Who wouldn't want to experience both small and big victories in their daily life? We all want to win in this "game" called life.

But victories don't come by accident.

You need a strategy if you want to win in life. And that strategy must include Jesus because He said that you can do nothing without Him. Your success in every aspect of life and your ability to live "the abundant life" are wrapped up in Him.

*"I am the vine; you are the branches. If you remain in Me and I in you, you will bear much fruit; apart from Me you can do nothing. John 15:5*

The tips in this book will show you what to incorporate into your daily routine so you can experience more of those victories. You'll discover that God is *for* you and not against you. He loves you and wants you to **live to win!**

Did you know that the God of the entire universe sustains your life? He loves you with a "no matter what" kind of love. No matter what you've done or haven't done, He will always love you. And because He loves you, He only wants the best for you. His desire is to give you anything and everything that is good so that you can enjoy life.

*We achieve this VICTORY through our faith.*
1 John 5:4

But the enemy of your success would like nothing better than to distract you and make you think that you don't matter to God. Rest assured, God hears you, He sees you, and He cares about what you experience in life.

I have often wondered what it would be like to always win, to live with confidence that "good success" is, and will continue to be, my daily experience. So I asked God how that could happen. This is what He said:

*BELIEVE I LOVE YOU AND THAT MY PROMISES ARE TRUE FOR YOU.*

*ASK ME, THEN ACT AS IF YOU HAVE IT.*

*SPEAK MY WORD SO YOUR WORDS AGREE WITH MINE ABOUT YOUR VICTORY, FUTURE, AND PURPOSE.*

*EXPECT THAT I WILL DO WHAT I PROMISED.*

*STAND WITH AN ATTITUDE OF GRATITUDE ABOUT THE VICTORY THAT JESUS MADE SURE YOU'VE ALREADY WON.*

To help me remember these five essential principles, I use the acronym B.A.S.E.S.:

**B**ELIEVE

**A**SK and ACT as if

**S**PEAK

**E**XPECT

**S**TAND

This illustration can help you remember these principles:

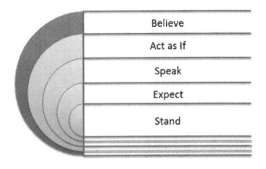

By using the tips, strategies, and worksheets in **Live to Win**, you'll gain a deeper and more meaningful understanding of how to experience the victory and rest that Jesus promised you.

> *"Come to me, all of you who are weary and carry heavy burdens, and I will give you rest."* Matthew 11:28 NLT

It's as if Jesus was lovingly saying:

> *"Come here to Me. You're weary and exhausted from carrying this burden and from your "do-it-yourself" life efforts. Let Me put an end to your frustration and fatigue. I don't want you constantly conscious of your sin, shame, and guilt. That's too heavy a load for you. I want you to be constantly conscious of My love and My grace. I want you to enjoy the freedom, the refreshing, and the restorative power that they bring. Rest in Me. Rest… to see My blessings manifest!*

This beckoning from Jesus was an imperative. He knew if we choose to come to Him, focus on His love for us, and exchange our weakness for His strength, we would see how He always upholds all His promises. He always honors the covenant that He established so that we can be fully assured of His love, presence, and willingness to act on our behalf. Then, we can rest in a position of victory,

Are you eager to put down all the heavy, awkward, and ineffective do-it-yourself tools you've been using to force life to be what you want it to be?

Are you open to replacing them with His lightweight, ergonomic, and powerfully effective tools of victorious grace?

In the following pages, you'll discover what they are and how to use them. They will empower you to make good success your daily experience so that you live like a champion.

*You* can **live to win**!

## LIVE TO WIN!

To succeed within God's plan, you have to learn to live by faith.
The Word is the point of origin of your faith.

www.EvangelineColbert.com

# 1

## CHAMPIONS BELIEVE THEY WIN

*"If you declare with your mouth, "Jesus is Lord," and **believe** in your heart that God raised him from the dead, you will be saved. For it is with your heart that you **believe** and are justified, and it is with your mouth that you profess your faith and are saved."*

Romans 10:9, 10

God has a system and everything works according to His system, whether or not we choose to adhere to it *and* whether we choose to believe it or not. Just like the law of gravity works for everyone whether they believe it or not, God's love for every human being exists, whether they believe He loves them or not.

His system for us to receive from Him requires that we believe that He is a loving Rewarder, not an unrelenting Punisher. This system to receive from God is based on Romans 10:9,10 (above). I believe these powerful verses are pivotal because they are the foundation for getting what you desire from God. Salvation is not only about going to heaven after death; it is also about your quality of life here on earth.

Scripture shows us that God wants only the best in life for us. His desire is to save us, keep us safe and sound, and to remain ever on-point to rescue us from danger or destruction while we live here on earth. That destruction does not only exist in the place of Hell after death; it exists during life on earth in the form of injury or peril, poverty, dysfunctional relationships, and suffering from disease.

God sent Jesus so that He could rescue us from *all* of that. His desire is to see us delivered, favored, prospering, made well, healed to wholeness, and restored. This is all made possible by believing in His Son, Jesus.

Romans 5:17 states, "We are to *reign in life* through the one Christ Jesus." Jesus desires for us to be victors and to reign in this life on earth, not to have to wait until we get to heaven. He wants us to hit a home run in life.

Here's an illustration: When you play the game of baseball, you have to have the right equipment when you step up to the plate. If you want to have a chance of hitting a home run, you have to have a bat to hit the ball. Stepping up to the plate with a roll of wrapping paper instead of a wooden bat will not make that ball go very far.

Similarly, playing the game of life in God's ballpark, you have to use the right equipment as well, and follow his principles in order to hit that home run in life. The equipment we use in God's ballpark is His Word, found in the Bible. When we use His Word, we are putting Him first, and we open ourselves to experience more of how He wants us to rest in Christ.

> *"Relax every strain, and lay off every burden. Let yourself go in a perfect abandonment of ease and comfort, sure that, since He holds you up, you are perfectly safe. Your part is simply to rest. His part is to sustain you; and He cannot fail."* ~Hannah Whitall Smith

You can **live to win** by climbing the proverbial ladder of success through your own effort or you can do so by resting— believing in the finished work that Jesus did on your behalf on the cross. It's the difference between taking the stairs to the top of a skyscraper and taking the elevator. Either way, you reach the top but getting there is much easier, less tiring, and faster via the elevator. When you choose to **live to win** by believing Jesus is your source of all things good, it's like taking a *spiritual* elevator.

The word "believe" means to have confidence in something or someone. Biblically, it means having a conviction that Jesus is able and willing to come to your rescue, that He is on your side. Belief is having confidence in the truth or reliability of something without having absolute tangible proof. This requires a personal buy-in, an acceptance that something exists, whether you are able to see it or not. "Belief "can be used interchangeably with "faith".

Believe that God loves you. That's first and foremost. God's nature is to always love. God *is* love and He wants you to believe His love is continually being poured out to you (1 John 4:8,16). Develop an intimate relationship with Him as you focus on His love for you and the favor that He pours out abundantly.

When you believe His love, you have confidence and boldness and there's no room for fear to overwhelm you! Keep believing God's Word. Keep believing God's Love.

*And we have come to know and to believe the love that God has for us. God is love, and the one who remains in love remains in God, and God remains in him.* 1 John 4:16

Believe that through His finished work on the cross, Jesus has already put you in a position of victory. You don't have to wait until you get to heaven; the victory is *already* yours.

In Luke 8:50, we're given an account of a man who had to believe, despite the very trying circumstances he was facing. Jairus was a father whose daughter was sick and near death. Jairus asked Jesus to come to his home and heal his daughter.

Jesus agreed but along the way stopped to minister to someone else. Jairus began getting a little nervous, thinking that time was running out. But Jesus said to him "fear not, believe only."

Why do you think Jesus told him that? Jairus was facing this dire situation regarding his daughter's life and Jesus was not moving quickly enough to get to her and heal her! Jairus didn't question Jesus' ability to heal but he might have begun to question the sincerity of Jesus, His attention to details, and even His love for him and his daughter.

*But Jesus needed Jairus to believe in His **willingness** despite the delay. He wanted him to know that delayed did not mean denied.*

He wanted Jairus to believe in His love for him and his daughter, in His willingness to help, and ultimately in His ability to help rectify Jairus' situation. Regardless of what delays you might experience, Jesus wants you to do the same thing— "fear not, believe only".

So when you think He's taking much too long to address your situation, remember there are some specific things He wants you to believe. He wants you to believe in His love, His *willingness*, and His ability.

## Wrong believing

> *"Unbelief is having a higher regard for yourself. Faith is having a higher regard for God." ~ Joseph Prince*

You are what you are, not because of what you've experienced but because of what you have chosen to believe about those experiences. Some people say, " I know God is able to do it, I just don't know if He's willing to do it for *me*."

Charles Capps, in his book, *Success Motivation*, states that God's willingness to get personally involved in our lives and to use His power on our behalf is multiplied through our knowledge of Him (2 Peter 1:2). He notes, "When you know God will, then He is willing. If you are in doubt about His willingness, He won't. Be convinced, by discovering His promises in His Word, that He is indeed willing to bring good things into your life."

Have you ever believed that God is the cause for your negative circumstances? The devil is actually the one that causes all the interjection of tragedy into your life. God wants you to experience only joy, peace, and goodness. When you believe God is the source of tragedy instead of your source of triumph, you are believing wrong.

So many times, especially during the trials of life, people blame God for their misfortunes and troubles. They tend to think that He is punishing them for something they did wrong.

But we are clearly shown in John 10:10 that it is the devil that comes into our circumstance to *kill* our dreams, *steal* our joy, and *destroy* our hope of anything good coming our way. Keep reading to the end of that verse and be encouraged by it—Jesus came to bring us life. He brings life to our dreams, life to our relationships, life to our finances, and life to our bodies and minds. He presents us with such an abundance of life that it overflows from us to others, enabling us to reach out and help others **live to win**. The way you think about Jesus is important. Your thought-life greatly influences how you experience life.

Your repeated thoughts inevitably give rise to your words. Your words will bring positive energy (life) or negative energy (death) to your circumstances (Proverbs 18:21). They influence the decisions you make and the actions you take. Your actions will aggregate to become your habits. Your habits will shape your character.

This is the thread that connects your beliefs to your character and determines the lifestyle you live—whether you **live to win** or live to lose. When you believe wrong, you will begin to speak wrong (negative) words and your consistently wrong words will eventually lead you to wrong choices and wrong actions.

Wrong believing interferes with your ability to accept and

possess what belongs to you through the finished work of Jesus. Guilt and self-condemnation frequently get in the way. But Romans 8:1 helps you see that believing that God condemns you is *wrong* believing:

> *"Therefore, no condemnation now exists*
> *for those in Christ Jesus."*

This is your truth only because Jesus did the ultimate good thing on your behalf. He died to give you a new position, a position of victory that comes with a clear conscience and a great inheritance. Because of that, you can choose to believe God's words, His promises, and that good things are coming your way.

Believing His words will transform your fear into faith and your tragedy into triumph. Let His Word be a tool you use, your personal hammer, to chisel away and break into pieces the stubborn things that bind you in the grip of fear and unbelief (Jeremiah 23:29).

"Is not **My Word** like fire"—this is the LORD's declaration—

"and like a **hammer** that *pulverizes* rock?"

Jeremiah 23:29

www.EvangelineColbert.com

A crucial building block of your belief system is hearing the word of God over and over again. God has made promises about your family, your finances, your peace of mind, your safety, your health, and your future. If you want to believe the promises of God, you need to hear them. Romans 10:17 reinforces this. It informs us that faith, which is believing in the existence of a thing, comes by hearing what God says about the matter.

Your present-day experience was created by what you thought and believed up until today. Your thoughts and beliefs became the foundation of your life experience. Likewise, your future is being created by what you are doing *today*—by what you believe, what you ask God for, what you speak, what you expect from God, and by what you show gratitude for.

You can change how your life is being played out simply by changing what you believe! It is up to you to decide to build your belief based on the promises of all the good things God has planned for you.

Zig Ziglar, a world-renowned motivational speaker said, "You are *what you are* and *where you are* because of what has gone into your mind. You can change *what you are* and *where you are* by changing what goes into your mind."

Remember, what goes into your mind determines what you believe. What you believe determines who you are, what you have, and what you do. Beliefs evolve when you allow yourself to move past fears and discover freedom and the victories awaiting you on the other side.

## Right Believing

Believe that God the Father loves you just like He loves Jesus. That's something that I've only been learning in recent years, because I always thought Jesus was JESUS, so how could God possibly love me like He loves Him? But John 17:23 says otherwise. It reveals that *God the Father loves us just as much as He loves Jesus.* It's imperative that we believe that this tiny but very important piece of God's Word is true.

Will you believe that God's word is *your* truth? Believe that it is the seed you need in order to have a future filled with multiple victories. God's Word contains the power you need for victory, and the way you tap into that power is through hearing and believing what God has said.

Believe that Jesus' work on the cross was perfect. Through His perfectly obedient life, He satisfied every requirement of God. God the Father accepted Jesus' obedience on behalf of all mankind. In our stead, Jesus also took upon Himself *all* of God's wrath that was kindled by *our* disobedience. In one felled swoop, He cleared away all the punishment that we deserved by taking it upon Himself on the cross.

*"He has done this through the death on the cross of his own human body, and now as a result Christ has brought you into the very presence of God, and you are standing there before him with nothing left against you—nothing left that he could even chide you for; the only condition is that you fully believe the Truth, standing in it steadfast and firm, strong in the Lord, convinced of the Good News that Jesus died for you, and **never shifting from trusting Him** to save you."*
*Colossians 1:22,23 TLB*

God is not angry with us anymore. Because of Jesus' perfect work, we don't have to endure God's anger. Proof of that is also found in I Thessalonians 5:9 NLT: "for God chose to save us, through our Lord Jesus Christ, not to pour out his anger on us." God's love is intentional. He wants us to receive loving salvation, not angry condemnation (John 3:17).

We must know about *and* believe God's love for us. We can know about something and not believe it is for us. Belief is a means of taking ownership by having full confidence, being fully persuaded, and having a "resting" trust in what you know to be real. Belief is beyond mere mental assent.

Mental assent says, "It's true because it's in the Bible." Belief (faith) says, "That promise is true for *me* because Jesus loves *me*." For example, you can know that your spouse loves you (mental assent) but until you believe it (trust and rest in it as your truth), you are susceptible to doubt and wondering if your spouse is cheating.

You don't have to work hard at believing. Jesus has said that He wants you to experience rest with Him so you can enjoy life's ride! You can find joy in knowing that God has gone ahead of you to prepare the way to your destination. The destination is good and so is His plan for getting you there.

*For I know the plans I have for you," declares the LORD, "plans to prosper you and not to harm you, plans to give you hope and a future.*
Jeremiah 29:11 NIV

You have a choice in the journey: to enjoy getting there by resting in Him or by worrying and being fearful of what could possibly happen.

For example, everybody on a roller coaster is going to the same destination. But at the end, some people were so afraid and tense throughout the entire ride that they could not enjoy it and got off never wanting to try it again. Others, who threw their arms up, smiled, and kept their eyes open because they chose to relax and enjoy the ride, are more likely to get off wanting to try the ride again.

Become carefree by looking to and trusting in Jesus' goodness. Rest, knowing that everything is not on your shoulders because you've given it to Him. Just focus on the thought, "God's got this."

*I had **believed** to see the goodness of the Lord. I look eagerly for*
*Him to do good things in my life.*
Psalm 27:13,14 [paraphrased]

## Jesus as Your Pinch Hitter

In baseball, the pinch hitter comes in as a substitute for a player
that has gotten injured, is tired, or is not performing well. They
finish the remainder of the game for that player. Maybe you
could think of it this way: Jesus became your pinch hitter and
took on all the wrath and punishment that you should have
endured.

So, if Jesus steps in as your pinch hitter, imagine He would say,
"Go stand over there, I've got this. Watch me and rest, trusting
that I'm going to do a great job of taking care of things out there
in the field of life." Wouldn't you enjoy resting, knowing that
He's working on your behalf?

How do you empower yourself to believe these things that God
says Jesus did on our behalf so that you can enjoy life? Again, it
boils down to using the right equipment, and that equipment is
the Bible. Spend time in God's Word—making sure that as
you're reading it you're also *hearing* it. Faith comes as a
consequence of repeatedly hearing the promises and words of
God.

The Word is the point of origin of your faith. Faith proceeds out
of the Word as your physical ears and your spiritual ears hear it.

As we hear the Word, we experience the empowerment that God wants us to have in our lives. This is especially true when we are hearing the Word coming out of our own mouth.

John G. Lake, a pastor known for his great faith in the 1800's, once said, "sometimes the difficulty is not in believing the Word of God, but the difficulty is getting away from some of the things that will settle in our own hearts and minds as being facts, although they were untrue."

Many times we have old mind-tapes running in our thoughts. It's usually something negative that someone said to us. It doesn't necessarily have to be something a parent said; it could have been a teacher, a friend, or even someone you don't know that said something that injured you spiritually, and you're still thinking that way about yourself.

Those words other people said to you as a child or even as an adult influence how you see yourself today. But God says, "No, that's not how I see you. I see you differently." Renew your mind to this and change what you are thinking about yourself so that it is in alignment with how He sees you. Find out from the Bible how God sees you. He sees you through a lens of love and He wants you to view yourself in the same manner. See yourself as being loved by the God who is so great and powerful that He sustains the entire universe.

*"Believe in the Lord your God and you will be able to stand firm... and you will be successful."*
*2 Chronicles 20:20 NIV*

## Holy Spirit—Your Life Coach

To succeed within God's plan, you have to learn to live by faith. Much like a life coach who helps a client make positive changes in their life, the Holy Spirit is also coaching us. He's letting us know that we've got to change how we think and what we believe in order to live life purposefully and to the best of our ability. And what are the benefits of doing that?

If you are repeatedly reminding yourself of those positive and purposeful things, they become a part of you, as if you're on autopilot. Repetition empowers your mind to make a shift so that believing—being certain about a God-promised outcome— becomes automatic.

When you renew your mind to the Word of God, along with the practical and helpful insights the Holy Spirit brings, you will live a life of greater victory, power, and favor. This is what becomes your new normal, your new way of believing and living.

This new way of believing is based upon having confidence that God has said, "Yes" to *everything* He has promised. His promises are certain. You can confidently count on His fulfillment of them.

*"For no matter how many promises God has made, they are*
*"Yes" in Christ. And so through Him the "Amen"*
*is spoken by us to the glory of God."*
2 Corinthians 1:20 NIV

## A Few Good Promises to Believe

Renew your mind to these promises God has made so that you can believe you will **live to win**!

**He has promised to love you:**

> John 17:23b ESV - *that the world may know that You sent Me and loved them even as You loved Me.*

> 1John 4:16 ESV - *So we have come to know and to believe the love that God has for us. God is love, and whoever abides in love abides in God, and God abides in him.*

> 1 John 4: 18 NIV - *There is no fear in love. But perfect love drives out fear, because fear has to do with punishment.*

**He has promised to *not* withhold His goodness from you:**

> Psalm 84:11 HNV - *For the LORD God is a sun and a shield. The LORD will give grace and glory. He withholds no good thing from those who walk blamelessly.*

**He has promised to see you as blameless and to not condemn or punish you:**

> Romans 8:1 NLT - *So now there is no condemnation for those who belong to Christ Jesus.*

1 Thessalonians 5:9 NLT - *For God chose to save us through our Lord Jesus Christ, not to pour out his anger on us.*

2 Corinthians 5:21 NIV – *For God made Christ, who never sinned, to be the offering for our sin, so that we could be made right with God through Christ.*

**He has promised to never remember your sins:**

Hebrews 8:12 HCSB—*For I will be merciful to their wrongdoing, and I will never again remember their sins.*

## Limited Faith = Doubt

Jesus wants you to believe in Him. He had many experiences with those who followed Him and did not believe. For instance, His disciples had multiple opportunities to believe Jesus had risen without actually seeing Him. They had a chance to believe it by faith and not by sight. It took a while, but finally all of them believed that He had risen, except "Doubting Thomas." He was the epitome of a Christian with limited faith.

Limited faith is controlled by outward circumstances and is motivated by fear. Trials don't bring faith—the Word brings faith. The Lord works with and confirms the Word (Mark 16:20) so that we can know that His Word works and we can rely on it. Jesus' words always act as a means to kindle hope and raise the level of our faith. He wants us to have confidence in Him and in what He has said. He does not want us to doubt Him.

Doubt is always a product of deceit and a consequence of distance. Doubt arises due to our being deceived into thinking that God is not on our side in the midst of our trouble. It increases when we have distanced ourselves from the Word; it also minimizes the role and efficacy of our prayer. It infiltrates our circumstances and reduces our trust because we are distracted from God's promises. *Doubt is our automatic response when we don't look to Jesus and keep our focus fixed on His love for us.*

Faith says Yes. Fear says No.

The story of King Ahaz illustrates how unbelief and reliance on people, instead of on God, can lead to undesirable consequences. Isaiah chapter seven is the account of an enemy's plan to attack the people of God. Verses 7 and 9 get to the heart of what God had to say about the enemy's plan and the faith of the people of Judah:

> *But this is what the Sovereign Lord says:*
> *"This invasion will never happen;*
> *it will never take place…[but] unless your faith is firm, I cannot make you stand firm."*

Full faith in the promise given in Isaiah 7:7 would have enabled Ahaz to dispense with all his earthly plans to call on the aid of any "arm of flesh." God had already set the stage for Ahaz to trust and believe Him. He clearly explained, *"If you don't take your stand in faith, you won't have a leg to stand on"* Isaiah 7:9 (MSG). Doubt and distrust of God's promise led Ahaz to take steps that did not establish him on solid ground. Instead, his decision made his position even more insecure and unstable.

> *"When I do the believing, God does the achieving."*
> ~ Jerry Savelle

## What to Believe

It is up to you to build your belief in the good things God has planned for you. Because He loves you, He has already provided every good thing to you through his Son, Jesus. It's your choice to believe in His no-matter-what kind of love. Believing this love is the foundation of receiving those good things.

Hebrews 11:6 gives us insight into this—without faith or belief in what Jesus has freely given you and promised you, it is impossible to please or agree with Him. God is a Rewarder! Those who diligently seek him and believe that His Word is true in their personal situations are the ones who will receive what his word has promised.

Believe that God's desire is for you to live above the things you currently struggle with, even to live without the things you struggle with. Jesus came to give you life more abundantly, life that overflows with favor. He wants you to enjoy his blessings in every area of your life. You can begin to do this by simply being more conscious of Jesus' love for you.

## Believe the Lover's Love

*I have loved you with an everlasting love; therefore, I have continued to extend faithful love to you.* Jeremiah 31:3 HCSB

God *is* love. Love eagerly pursues us. It longs for us and desires us. It wants more than companionship—it desires and delights in intimacy. Love is verdant, alive, always germinating, always producing fruit—joy, peace, patience, gentleness, and more. (Galatians 5:22,23). Get to know and believe the love God has for *you*.

Real love—God's love— is continual, long and drawn out; it's forever moving forward and always giving to others. As you believe His love on a deeper, more personal level, you'll find your faith flows more easily.

Faith is being firmly assured of God's love, knowing that He will do what He said He would do. It is being intentional about trusting Him to keep His promises. Here's a helpful acronym to help you easily remember what faith is:

**Faith** = **F**irmly **A**ssured and **I**ntentionally **T**rusting **H**im

Jesus said, "When you team up with and rely only upon men, the thing you desire is impossible. But when you team up with and rely only upon God, *all* things are possible (Mark 10:27, paraphrased)." In this passage the word "with" means "in close proximity to."

So if you read that Scripture again, it takes on a whole new meaning. It's as if God was saying, "If you are relying on yourself and other people to make something happen, it'll be impossible. But if you trust Me and stay in close proximity to Me so that you and I can do this together, all things are possible. "

Remember, doubt is a consequence of distance. Conversely, trust is the consequence of closeness. Nearness allows trust to emerge. That's why God beckons us in to draw near to Him (James 4:8).

Trust is the result when we increasingly draw near to God through His Word and prayer. Trust infiltrates our circumstances and erases our doubt when we focus on and verbally affirm His promises. Trust is our automatic response when we have practiced looking to Jesus in the Word and acknowledging His love for us. Belief confidently agrees with and trusts in God's plan.

Jesus challenged Martha to believe in the midst of a seemingly hopeless situation—the death of her brother Lazarus (John 11:40). He said, "If you would believe, you would see." This is totally contrary to what most folks think today. They are determined not to believe until they see! But, Martha believed and waited expectantly to see the works of God and she was not disappointed. Lazarus was raised from the dead. Martha's belief came before Martha's seeing.

Martha made a decision to trust Jesus' instruction to believe that He would change her circumstances even thought she didn't yet see a change. His words compelled her to trust that she would see something good happen if she would believe In His love, power, and willingness. Most people think, "I'll believe it when I see it." God wants us to think, "I'll see it because I believe it!"

Let's revisit the account of Jairus again because Jesus gave him a similar instruction. Jairus sought out Jesus to come see and heal his daughter. His daughter was on the verge of dying (Luke 8:41). Along the way back to his home, a servant came and told Jairus it was useless to bring Jesus because his daughter had died. But upon hearing this news, Jesus encouraged Jairus, to "fear not, only believe."

Here's where we see that it's never useless to bring Jesus into our circumstances! *After believing* that Jesus would handle his problem, Jairus *saw* the miraculous result—Jesus brought his daughter back to life *and* made her completely well.

In another Scripture, a disciple of Jesus set conditions on his belief in the miraculous. John 20:24-31 gives the account of

"Doubting Thomas" saying to the other disciples, "If I can see and touch Him, then I'll believe [that Jesus has risen]."

His belief was based on what he could do, and what he could experience in the natural realm with his senses. It was a lost opportunity to have, show, and exercise his faith. Jesus appeared and challenged Thomas to not be faithless and unbelieving but instead to continually believe. Jesus knew that without faith, Thomas would be limited to the very narrow world of the natural realm comprehended by his senses and not experience the supernatural blessings that belief in Jesus' resurrection could bring.

Do you think fear was a factor in Thomas' doubt? Are *you* afraid to believe? Faith is how we make contact with God. It keeps us aware of His love, power, and favor.

Faith involves seeing the invisible with the mind.

> *"Faith led Moses to leave Egypt and he was not*
> *afraid of the king's anger.*
> *Moses didn't give up but **continued as if he could***
> ***actually see the invisible God."***
> Hebrews 11:27 GW

Faith requires the mind to look to Jesus with perseverance. If the mind is cluttered with negative thoughts, it is distracted from looking to Jesus and therefore, faith gets diminished.

> *"Faith proves to the mind the reality of things that cannot be seen by the bodily eye."* ~ Matthew Henry

Jesus wanted Thomas to believe and act as if he could actually see the invisible God. This was His desire because He knew that without faith, it is impossible to please God (Hebrews 11:6).

How can you "act as if" you can see someone that is invisible?

How can you act as a champion even before you experience victory? As in sports, becoming and remaining a champion in life requires some preparation and conditioning.

Take a moment right now to do some Champion Conditioning— assess your belief system before moving on to the next chapter.

*Believe* you win!

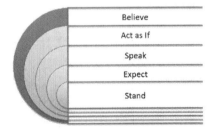

# *CHAMPION CONDITIONING*
## Believe to Win

Write a statement regarding what you believe about Jesus' love for *you* today.

Now, ask God, "What *should* I believe about You and Your love for me?" and record your thoughts.

***AFFIRMATION:*** *I live to win by believing that God loves me like He loves Jesus and that His wisdom empowers me to win.*

NOTE: An affirmation is a definitive statement that you vocalize. It is something that you declare is already existent, even if you're not currently experiencing it. *Effective* affirmations are positive statements, specifically crafted around the promises found in God's Word and they are framed in the present tense. Creating personal affirmations based on God's Word is a way of increasing your belief that His promises are true.

You'll do more with affirmations in Chapter 3.

# LIVE TO WIN!

Most people think,
"I'll believe it when I
see it."
God wants us to
think, "I'll see it
because I believe it!"

www.EvangelineColbert.com

# 2

## ASK, THEN ACT AS IF YOU'VE WON

*Keep on asking, and you will receive what you ask for. Keep on seeking, and you will find. Keep on knocking, and the door will be opened to you.* Matthew 7:7 NLT

If you're feeling unworthy and unnoticed, ask God to give you a fresh revelation of His love. He will be thrilled with your request! Knowing how much He loves you will empower you. You'll grow to be more confident of who you are in Him. There will be an increase of the instances where you experience His favor. Yes, all of this will happen because you've attained a greater knowledge of His no-matter-what love for *you*. But first, you must ask.

✝

Before you read anything else about asking God for something, let's make sure you've asked Him for the most important thing you could ever request from Him. Have you asked Jesus into your heart, to become your Savior? If not, pray this simple prayer out loud to start a new life with Him:

**Dear God, I come to You in the Name of Jesus. I admit that I am not right with You, and I want to be right with You. I ask You to forgive me of all my sins. I invite Jesus to rule and reign in my heart from this day forward. I believe with my heart and I confess with my mouth that Jesus is my Lord and Savior. Make me the person you want me to be. In Jesus' Name I pray. Amen.**

If this is the first time you've prayed a prayer of salvation, heaven is rejoicing! Jesus has come into your life and His Holy Spirit now resides in you forever. You are a new creation, no longer dead to God. You are now a child of God, positioned for victory because of His love as your Father. Now you can ask with confidence.

I encourage you to tell someone the good news about this significant change in your life. Read the Victory Verses that are in the Appendix of this book. Also, look for a church that will teach you from God's Word how to live victoriously.

✝

When Jesus instructed us to "keep on asking" in Matthew 7:7, I believe that it was not a command to repeatedly ask for the same thing as if He didn't hear us the first time. It's more about how He always wants us to come to Him, no matter the situation, nor how dire the need. He wants us to always look to Him, knowing that He is our ultimate supplier of all that we need. We can never come to Him too often or ask for too much!

Maybe asking for what you want is similar to ordering something from an online store. You wouldn't place the order over and over again until it arrived at your residence and you held it in your hand. You'd place the order once, confident that the warehousing agent would send it your way and eventually you'd receive it.

Jesus wanted us to know that we could come to the Father at any time for any thing—with confidence. No matter how much we need, He wants to be our Source, the One who supplies our every need. His supply never runs out. By confidently believing that He would not withhold any good thing from us, we can ask according to His Word *in faith*. Then we can rest, assured that He has sent just the thing (healing, finances, enjoyable relationships, successful career, etc.) that we need.

In John 16:24 (NIV), Jesus reveals the principle of asking and points out *how* He wants us to ask:

*Until now you have not asked for anything in my name. Ask and you will receive, and your joy will be complete.*

Here's my modern-day interpretation of that scripture:

"Before now you have demanded nothing in my name, in the authority that I carry and in the integrity of my character. But now, I want you to make a demand for what is due you. Using My authority that I have given to you, make a demand on the things that I gave you the right to have, because I valued you as being worth dying for. Get a hold of them and then take them! That way your cheerfulness will be complete, every area of your life will be influenced by the joy of having what I gave you as a rightful heir of the Father.

I have not placed My blessings beyond your reach. Ask Me for what you need and want. Call for my favor. Live requiring my favor as a vital necessity of life. Search for the nuggets of great words that are hidden in my Word and then use them as you make your requests. Consider them as your tool for your urgent need that only I can satisfy."

We are not asking a favor of Jesus but rather making a demand of what's due to us—because of the authority He gave us. We can do so as a result of His finished work on the cross and through His resurrection. Let me be clear, "demand" does *not* imply that you're commanding God to do something. It means to call for those things that have already been made ours through Jesus' sacrifice. It means to call for those things that are not already in this physical realm and to speak about them as though they already can be seen. We do so by praying to the Father *in Jesus' authority*.

God's system requires that we step out of the world system, and by faith, step into His supernatural system and call for those things that are due to us because of Jesus' finished work. Those things will not just fall out of the sky; they will not magically happen or appear when we beg or cry for them. They will come to us when we use our faith to ask for them—being secure about who we are in Christ, secure enough to ask and believe that they are already ours. After all, it is faith that pleases God and puts us in agreement with His plan.

## The Power of *His* Words In Your Prayers

Jesus said, "If you remain in Me and My words abide in you, ask whatever you wish, and it will be done for you" (John15:7 NIV). If you have His words abiding in you, you can expect Him to do what you ask. It will be helpful to you to find scriptures that relate to your circumstances and meditate on them until you believe them—until they become real to you. That way, if the problem persists for a while, you'll be able to fight doubt because you've got His words still working in you and your circumstances.

Does your prayer ever need to degenerate to a manipulative system of begging? No! God does not withhold anything within his bountiful storehouse. As the ultimate loving parent, He doesn't withhold anything that would be advantageous to the life of His children. Jesus' name is our passport that gives us access to all that the Father has. His name gives us a prevailing victory so that we can **live to win** every day.

As the Father, God enjoys doing good things for His children. Believe that He is good; trust Him by asking Him for anything you need. Isn't that what most earthly fathers desire—that their children would freely come to them, wanting them to provide for their needs?

> *"There is no failure in receiving from God when faith does not break down."* ~Anonymous

## How to Ask and Receive

Ask God, knowing He's the One who loves you like no other. Ask Him with confidence that He is not only *able* to meet your needs but He is also *willing* to do so in abundance. God is Spirit and He tells us that He has ears that hear with excellent clarity (Psalm 27:7). When you call to Him, He hears you. He always keeps His promises and His power and goodness are always available—just ask!

Scripture says in 1 John 5:14 that when we ask anything according to His will, He hears us. The Bible is His will. So if God said it in the Bible, you can ask Him for it in Jesus' name, and you can have confidence that He has heard you. Verse 15 goes on to say that if we know that He has heard us, then we can know that we have what we have asked of Him.

I am God and there is no other!
I publicly proclaim
**bold promises**.
I do not whisper obscurities in
some dark corner so that no
one can know what I mean.
Ask me for what I said I would
give! For I speak only truth;
I always do what I say.
**I keep my promises!**

Isaiah 45:19 [paraphrased]

www.EvangelineColbert.com

*The key here is to ask according to His Word.* Have faith that His promises are for you personally. He has already provided and supplied what He said in the finished work of Jesus on the cross. It's up to you to accept it, to believe it, to receive it, to take hold of it, and not let go until you see it manifested.

*" And how bold and free we then become in His presence, freely asking according to his will, sure that he's listening. And if we're confident that he's listening, we know that what we've asked for is as good as ours. "* 1 John 5:14-15 MSG

Ask, because you believe that Jesus is the One who loves you like no other. Ask, knowing that He has promised and is willing to keep all His promises. Tom Brown, in his article, *How to Get Your Prayers Answered*, shares that "God's Word *is* His will. If you want to know what God's will is, then look at His Word. He only promises the things that He's willing to do. By not knowing His Word, delays in answers may make us think that God is denying us the answers. But by knowing the Word, delays are simply opportunities to stand on God's Word in faith."

## Dream Big, Ask Big

Dare to ask for big things like Jabez did, even though the Bible shows us his life's story had been tinged with pain. Here are the big things he asked God to do:

*"Oh that you would bless me indeed, enlarge my territory, that*
*Your hand would be with me,*

*and that You would keep me from evil."* ~ 1 Chronicles 4:10

Notice some of the key words that Jabez used in his one-sentence prayer—bless me, enlarge, *Your* hand, keep me. He recognized God's power. Jabez was confident that God could change his situation. He knew what he wanted from God and was not afraid to ask. He did not want to continue living a pain-filled life even though his name meant exactly that; "Jabez" meant "pain".

His mother named him that because she bore him with sorrow during her pregnancy or childbirth. The Bible does not record anything about this man anywhere else other than in this brief passage. God must have thought that Jabez chose his words wisely in this prayer because Jabez's request released the miraculous in his life—God granted what Jabez asked for.

Keywords are still important when asking for something. In today's job market, an applicant typically asks for a job by submitting a job application electronically through the Internet. Résumé and career experts strongly suggest that an applicant use the same key words and key phrases that the company's website uses in its job description.

This is because the company's search for a candidate involves algorithms that drive the search engine to look for those same words on each application. It's how they optimize finding the best candidates to hire.

God is much like that. He's looking for those who will agree with what He said. He's looking for people willing to identify themselves by speaking His words of life, who choose to use the same keywords and key phrases as those contained in His promises. He's looking for those who will *act* on the knowledge they have of His power and His love. He's looking for you to ask.

## Be Specific About What You Ask For

*Do not be anxious or worried about anything, but in everything [every circumstance and situation] by prayer and petition with thanksgiving,*
*continue to make your [**specific**] requests known to God.*
Philippians 4:6 AMP

My husband has always encouraged our children to ask him for whatever they need. He made it clear that they would need to tell him *specifically* what they needed. What is it that you want? It's important when you pray to ask God specifically for what you desire and then stand on His promises and watch Him work. When you're specific in asking for something, you have it clear in your mind what to expect.

You may want to begin to think about the kind of experience you want to have once your desire is manifested. Then, ask God for it. Perhaps you want a promotion on your job but you've seen how your co-workers have compromised their integrity in order to get ahead. You choose to stand in your integrity and not compromise.

You may want to specifically ask God for favor with your boss and to give you wisdom about how you can show your abilities to do your job in excellence and with a good attitude. Proverbs 16:3 may be just the ticket to that promotion—"Commit your works to the Lord and your plans will be established and succeed."

You can **live to win** without compromising your values. Success will be yours when you ask God for wisdom, to show you how to do it, and to order your steps according to His Word.

*Now if any of you lacks wisdom, he should ask God, who gives to all generously and without criticizing, and it will be given to him.*
James 1:5 HCSB

After seeing my best friend have a very hard time with morning sickness, I specifically asked God to allow me to have a pregnancy without it. I had no symptoms of morning sickness in any of my three pregnancies. You see, you don't *have to* experience things the way everyone else does.

Maybe you experience health issues as a result of being overweight. Make a decision and be determined to get healthy. Ask God to show you what you need to do and to help you do the things necessary to get to a *healthy* weight. Purpose in your heart to lose a *specific* amount of weight, in a *specific* amount of time, so that your health improves. Then take action to make it happen.

Find scriptures that encourage you on whatever you're specifically asking God for. Take His promises to heart as if He was speaking them directly to you (because He is) and then stand and act on them, believing they will come to pass.

Persevere in speaking those promises so your faith in them is established by hearing them.

*So then faith comes from what is heard, and what is heard comes through the message about Christ.*
Romans 10:17 HCSB

Whatever you ask God for, be specific, find His promise about it, and then think about that promise, believe it, act on it, speak it, and expect it. Joshua 1:8 says, "to do these things daily"—in other words, consistently. Consistency is key when dealing with the things of God. Isaiah 55:11 tells us the benefit of consistency—God's Word will not return to Him void (it will not be useless or of no effect), but it will accomplish what He sent it to do in your life [paraphrased].

Be specific and consistent. This will give you confidence in the vision you have for improved health, finances, relationships, and more. Your vision will not be empty or lifeless when you connect it to God's promises. Bathe your vision of a better life in the life changing anointing of His words. When you:

> ~ are specific in what you ask of God,
>
> ~ connect that desire to His promises,
>
> ~ speak that Word consistently, and
>
> ~ believe it will come to pass because of His grace,

He ensures the power of what He has said will accomplish what He desires in your life.

Frame your requests according to what He has promised in His Word, then you'll know you're asking according to His will. The easiest way to do this is to make a list of scriptures that show the promises that pertain to your situation. How do you find those scriptures? Think about keywords that relate to your situation— for example, healing, finances, temptations, marriage—and look them up in a Bible concordance. The concordance will show you verses related to your keywords.

Use the phrases in those scriptures to frame your prayer, knowing that you are now praying the will of God.

> A Prayer of Faith: *God, I thank you that your love for me is unconditional. It does not depend on what I do or don't do. Your love for me is so deep and wonderful! Thank you that through your Son, Jesus, I can ask you for anything in your Word. By faith, I*

*receive every blessing you have for me. I choose to believe your Word and speak and act as if I have already received Your blessings. I have confidence that You keep your promises. In Jesus' name, Amen.*

## Jehoshaphat Had to "Act as If"

In 2 Chronicles 20:12-17 (AMP), we see King Jehoshaphat preparing for battle against an enemy that far outnumbered his soldiers. He prayed, *"We have no might to stand against this great company that is coming against us. We do not know what to do, but our eyes are upon You."* That passage goes on to describe what happened next:

> *And all Judah stood before the Lord, with their children and their wives. Then the Spirit of the Lord came upon Jahaziel...a Levite of the sons of Asaph, in the midst of the assembly. He said, Hearken, all Judah, you inhabitants of Jerusalem, and you King Jehoshaphat. The Lord says this to you: Be not afraid or dismayed at this great multitude; for the battle is not yours, but God's. Tomorrow go down to them. Behold, they will come up by the Ascent of Ziz, and you will find them at the end of the ravine before the Wilderness of Jeruel. You shall not need to fight in this battle; take your positions, stand still, and see the deliverance of the Lord [Who is] with*

*you, O Judah and Jerusalem. Fear not nor be dismayed. Tomorrow go out against them, for the Lord is with you.*

Notice the instruction to "take your position, stand still, and see the deliverance of the Lord who is with you." To take position means to set oneself or to station oneself. The implication is to choose to stand with God. It provokes us to have an attitude of perseverance, to stand firm and remain in our covenant position with God when dealing with life's battles.

That's what Jehoshaphat did. He stood firm in his position of covenant with God and directed the people of his kingdom to do likewise. He called his people to worship the Lord, to praise Him with a loud voice, and to go out the next day with confidence that God would do what He said He would do. And God did indeed keep His word as we see this scene unfold in 2 Chronicles 20:20-26 (AMP):

*And they rose early in the morning and went out into the Wilderness of Tekoa; and as they went out, Jehoshaphat stood and said, Hear me, O Judah, and you inhabitants of Jerusalem! Believe in the Lord your God and you shall be established; believe... remain steadfast to His prophets and you shall prosper.*

*When he had consulted with the people, he appointed singers to sing to the Lord and praise Him in their holy priestly garments as they went out before the army, saying, Give thanks to the Lord, for His mercy and loving-kindness endure forever!*

*And when they began to sing and to praise, the Lord set ambushments against the men of Ammon, Moab, and Mount Seir who had come against Judah, and they were self-slaughtered;*

*For, suspecting betrayal, the men of Ammon and Moab rose against those of Mount Seir, utterly destroying them. And when they had made an end of the men of Seir, they all helped to destroy one another.*

*And when Judah came to the watchtower of the wilderness, they looked at the multitude, and behold, they were dead bodies fallen to the earth, and none had escaped!*

*When Jehoshaphat and his people came to take the spoil, they found among them much cattle, goods, garments, and precious things which they took for themselves, more than they could carry away, so much they were three days in gathering the spoil.*

*On the fourth day they assembled in the Valley of Beracah. There they blessed the Lord. So the name of the place is still called the Valley of Beracah blessing.*

Jehoshaphat believed what God had said and then he *acted* as if what God had said was true. He got into position—he and his people stood still—and watched God work. Their actions reflected confidence and trust in the Lord. Jehoshaphat did what seemed unwise in the natural. He knowingly took his people to a battle where they were outnumbered.

But, he recognized that he and his people were in covenant with God. The Lord could be trusted to keep His word and to fight the battle for them. They praised God for that.

As a result, their enemies turned on themselves and destroyed each other before Jehoshaphat and his people could even get to the scene of the fight. They were already victorious *before* they arrived at the battlegrounds because they believed what God promised and acted as if God was on their side.

Let this encourage *you* to act on God's promises, especially when the situation appears impossible!

> *"The ultimate achievement is to defeat the enemy without ever coming to battle."* ~Sun Tzu

> *"Faith gives reality or substance to things hoped for; it is what enables us to feel and act as if they are real. They exert an influence over us as if we saw them."*
> ~Albert Barnes, Barnes Commentary

## Does Practice Really Make Perfect?

So often we hear, "practice makes perfect," especially in sports. But, practice does not make perfect; practice makes permanent. Why? If we practice doing the wrong thing, we will continue to do the wrong thing! We have to change the way we do things. We need to practice those fundamentals that God instructs us to do in His Word.

Just as coaches have players do fundamental drills over and over again, and teachers have students do the fundamental multiplication table repeatedly, we need to read, meditate, and speak God's Word over and over again to be able to believe it and then act as if it's true in our lives. That's how we incorporate His promises of good into our lives.

I remember when I would go to pick up my sons from basketball practice and they would talk about how their coach had made them run "suicides" (a running drill), and then move on to drills for free throws and shooting. All of that was to build up their

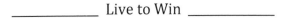

endurance, and to help them be more accurate in their shooting. More accurate shooting would lead to victory in the games against their opponents.

We are called to the same kind of thing so that we can endure and persevere until we achieve victory in this life. When we work on the fundamentals (believing God loves us, staying connected with Him through prayer, speaking His Word out loud, etc.), we can then *act* on them. By becoming more accurate in our focus— using God's Word to help us look to Jesus and all that He has provided for us— it's easier to arrive at our God-given destiny.

God does not desire, nor does he expect for you to simply give in and accept the fate of your circumstances. He wants you to anticipate receiving what you have asked of Him and then act as if it's already yours.

## Act and Speak As If the Unseen Exists

Below is an excerpt from my book, *A Seed of Hope: God's Promises of Fertility*, which is a devotional for women struggling with infertility. The thought here is applicable not only to infertility but to any situation where you're facing a challenge.

*Having confidence in what God says helps you to take action and to have courage to live as if what His Word promises you already exists. It actually does already exist in the spiritual realm. Your faith in what He has said about your circumstances is the means of accessing it so that it manifests in this natural realm.*

*You may have heard self-development teachers and speakers say if you want to be successful and prosperous, you need to "act as if" it's already so. That way of thinking actually lines up with Scripture and it's applicable to how you should live everyday. God does not desire nor expect you to live with or "accept the fate" of negative circumstances.*

*Abraham believed what God said to him about having a baby with his wife, Sarah, even though they were both over ninety years old. God is described as being the One who calls those things that be not as though they were.*

> *God in whom he believed, Who gives life to the dead and speaks of the nonexistent things that He has foretold and promised as if they already existed.* Romans 4:17 (AMP)

*In other words, God called forth and spoke about non-existent things "as if" they already existed. If that's God's way of doing things then, as a believer in Him, it should be your way of doing things too. After all, you are made in His image (Genesis 1:26).*

*Therefore, begin to act and speak "as if" your circumstances have already changed. Take action, having confidence that God loves you unconditionally and is keeping His promise that He will bless you.*

As you begin to *speak* as if your circumstances have changed because of the powerful influence of verbalizing God's Word with confidence, you'll begin to *see* that change you desire manifest.

Now, put some time into another phase of Champion Conditioning so you can ask God for wisdom and determine how you will *act* to win.

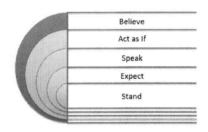

# *CHAMPION CONDITIONING*
## Act to Win

### Your Confidence in *Action*

**AFFIRMATION:** *I live to win by acting as if I am already a victor. I have all the benefits that Jesus died to give me in my health, finances, and relationships.*

What is the single greatest obstacle that hinders you from acting on what you believe?

Ask God for wisdom about how to overcome that obstacle (James 1:5; James 3:17).

List one specific thing you will do *today* to overcome that obstacle.

List three specific ways you can "act as if" you have already overcome it.

    1.

2.

3.

## Write and Pray a Word-Based Prayer

Using a note pad or journal—

> Find the scriptures that promise the answer to your need and are related to your situation. An online resource I use to find scriptures is www.blueletterbible.org.

> Write the scriptures that you've chosen. Writing helps you to connect those words with your inner thoughts.

> Write a personalized prayer request using keywords from those scriptures and insert your name in it.

> Determine in your heart that this matter is settled because God has addressed it in His Word (Psalm 119:89).

> Write a prayer of thanksgiving. Read it a few times to let it settle within you. Refer back to it regularly to remind you to act as if the answer is already yours.

Use this system as a way of developing Word-based prayers for any situation you may face. A Word-based prayer is an effective prayer!

## LIVE TO WIN!

Frame your requests according to what He has said/promised in His Word, then you'll know you're asking according to His will.

www.EvangelineColbert.com

# 3

---

# SPEAK LIKE A WINNER

## Speak the Promise, Not the Problem

*"Listen (consent and submit) to the words of the wise, and apply your mind to my knowledge: for it will be pleasant if you keep them in your mind [believing them]; your lips will be accustomed to [confessing] them. So that your trust (belief, reliance, support, and confidence) may be in the Lord."*
Proverbs 22:17,18 AMP

I am still learning how important my words are. Not only do they let others know what I think, but also they are actually vessels filled with the power to change things in my life *or* to keep things the same.

God framed the world using His words. He designed our universe to respond to words. He spoke words and **big** things happened (Genesis 1). That's why He sent the prophets of the Old Testament— to speak the words that He spoke so that those words would cause His plan to happen within this earth realm.

69

Throughout the Old Testament, we see so many prophetic words about what was coming in the future through the Messiah. Those prophecies proclaimed specific things to come. Those *words* would set the things in motion that God included in His plan for mankind. All of those words were eventually fulfilled, accomplished, and completed through Jesus.

God has placed that same significance and power in *our* words. Our words are able to frame and change our personal world when we speak what *God* says about our situation. The act of speaking what He has said initiates, strengthens, and builds our faith. Believing and speaking His promises instead of our problems can change our personal world.

If God said it, you can choose to believe it *and* you can choose to say it. The Apostle Paul encourages us to do so:

*"Just like the psalmist who wrote, "I believed it, so I said it," we **say** what we believe."* 2 Corinthians 4:13 MSG

Paul was conveying the thought that King David wrote in Psalm 116:10. David, known as a man who pursued the heart of God, encourages us to believe what God said, and then act on what we believe by speaking it.

Here are some tips about speaking the Word that should make it easier for you to develop this as a habit:

1. Find what God has said in the Bible about your circumstances—He only wants His best for you! Read it repeatedly to gain clarity.

2. Ask the Holy Spirit to give you a better understanding of that particular scripture.

3. Declare that scripture *daily* by making it a prayerful decree that's spoken out loud. Hear yourself confess the Word instead of all your troubling circumstances.

4. Humble yourself by putting aside your own point of view (what seems or appears like truth) and look at things the way God does.

5. Decide to speak what God has said about you and your circumstances during your everyday conversations.

His Word is Truth. Speak it and make it *your* truth. When you speak God's Word, you are releasing its power through your lips. Speaking it will help you believe what you say and you'll grow to speak it with greater faith.

## Affirm God's Promises

*I praise your name for your unfailing love and faithfulness; You have exalted Your name and Your promise above everything else.* Psalm 138:2 (paraphrased)

An affirmation is a definitive statement that you vocalize. It is about something that you declare is already existent, even if you're not currently seeing it or experiencing it with your other senses. *Effective* affirmations are positive statements, specifically crafted around the promises found in God's Word and they are framed in the present tense. Creating personal affirmations based on God's Word is a way of increasing your belief that His promises are true.

Speaking daily affirmations is even more powerful when you say them as if they are already true. When spoken with clarity and conviction, your emotions will make your affirmations come alive. When you first begin to speak your affirmations, your old beliefs may rear their ugly heads. But when you *speak the Word often*, you will renew your mind to it as your truth and essentially change the neural pathways in your brain. You will be empowered to "act as if" what you're affirming already exists even more strongly.

Dr. Caroline Leaf is a cognitive neuroscientist specializing in Neuropsychology. She explains in detail about the role of neural pathways in our brain and how they are influenced by our thoughts and words. She has done extensive research on the brain and emphasizes, "Every time you think and choose, you cause structural change in your brain. By controlling the direction of your mind, you control the direction of your life."

You become what you think about most. Why? Your thoughts will eventually become your spoken words. The things you repeatedly say and hear will eventually influence your actions. Your repeated actions will become your habits. Your habits will always be a clear indicator of your character.

www.EvangelineColbert.com

Your words have power! Even in your seemingly insignificant chats and conversations, your spoken words are shaping what you will experience that day and in the days ahead.

## Talking Loud and Saying Nothing

James Brown was an R&B singer known as the "King of Soul". He sang a song that had this line in its lyrics: "talking loud and saying nothing." His point in that song was that we can be so busy talking yet our words have no substance, depth, or positive efficacy to them.

Think about your daily conversations with family, co-workers, and friends. Would you be found guilty of talking loud and yet saying NOTHING? If you were speaking what God said in His Word about your circumstances, you would never be found guilty of that. If you were speaking His promises, you would be "talking loud saying *something*"—something of great substance and efficacy *every* time.

God created everything by speaking it into existence and everything that He created was good. The entire first chapter of Genesis is filled with instances of God speaking in order to create. Light, the universe, water, plants with regenerative seeds, and animals that could reproduce, all came into existence because God *said* it should be so. Nothing that He made was created without Him speaking it into existence.

It all started with Him saying, "Let there be light." He continued to say, "let there be…" until He was satisfied that what He had created was *all* "good" and ideally ready to be inhabited. He had prepared this world to be the perfect environment for His ultimate creation, Man, to live without any lack or brokenness.

Man was the only creature that came into existence through something in addition to God speaking. Man was created with God's words *and* His touch. Through His touch, God was showing His desire for relationship with mankind, to show His love for the ones made in His image. We are made in His image—beings who have creative power in their faith-filled spoken words.

Everything God desires to have happen has been spoken. At the time of Creation, He spoke, and it came to pass exactly as He said. And what came to pass was *always* good.

After the Fall of Man, God would use a prophet, priest, or king to speak what He wanted to appear and happen in this earth realm. Through His words being spoken by those men and women, He brought to pass the greatest miracle of all. Their words set the stage for the Son of God, Jesus, to make His appearance here on earth.

> *"Our words act as seeds and when planted by being spoken into our lives, they will produce a harvest. This applies to both the good and the bad things we speak about our lives. The result can be a harvest of weeds or a harvest of good things in our lives."*
> *~Evangeline Colbert*

Obviously, God finds it important that we speak His Word here on the earth. Proverbs 18 tells us that our words have the power and energy of life and also of death.

If we focus more on saying God's promises, faith will come and it will also increase. So use your words wisely! Use them to speak God's promises. Use them to bless yourself and others. Use them to bring goodness into this world. Use your words to bestow favor to yourself, your family, and to others.

*Death and life are in the power of the tongue.* Proverbs 18:21

## Speak Blessing

Spoken words program your life either for success or for defeat. Did you know that we can actually be trapped by our own words?

*You have been trapped by what you said, ensnared by the words of your mouth.* Proverbs 6:2

Live life being cognizant that your words can free you but they can also ensnare you. Purpose to go through each day speaking words of life, victory, and blessing!

A blessing is defined as a statement made to evoke and activate the good in our lives. It is the act of saying words filled with life and positivity. *It's wonderful to bless yourself.* Take time daily to declare your own blessings by speaking God's power-packed promises over your circumstances so that you program your life for success.

In the meantime, here's a good one to declare aloud right now—

*"The Lord's favor surrounds me as a shield."*
Psalm 5:12

Back in the time that the Psalmist wrote the fifth Psalm, the shields of soldiers were almost as tall as the men. Soldiers would huddle together and put their shields above and all around themselves to protect their group.

God's favor is like that in our lives; it surrounds us completely. It totally encompasses us. Bring God's favor to your troublesome situation—by finding promises in Scripture that are applicable to it. Read them to yourself out loud. No matter what difficulty you may be going through right now, there is something in God's Word that addresses it, brings life to it, and ultimately changes it for the better.

> *"Do not My words [continually and progressively] do good to him who walks uprightly?* Micah 2:7b

Or, if there is something good that you desire to come into your life, find a scripture that relates to it, and then begin to speak that to yourself. Even though you may not believe it at first, keep speaking the Word. If you have some doubts about it, persevere—keep speaking the Word.

Faith comes by repeatedly hearing God's Word (Romans 10:17), especially when you're hearing it from your own mouth—so keep speaking the Word. There's an added dimension of power when you're hearing God's Word spoken from your own mouth.

> *"Hearing yourself say something aloud is a powerful tool."* ~Valorie Burton

Here's an example of how to make a scripture verse into an affirmation. Second Corinthians 5:21 makes it clear that "we are made the righteousness of God in Christ Jesus." In affirming that scripture, you could say something like, "Thank you Father, that I am the righteousness of God in Christ, therefore, I am the right person at the right place at the right time, doing and saying the right things with the right people."

Being righteous is not some mystical, ethereal concept; being righteous is having been made to be in the state or condition that you *ought* to be, the one God intended you to be in all along. He has established you in Christ so that you are as you ought to be— *continually* and eternally righteous in His sight. That's why, as a believer in Jesus, you are now right with God.

I've heard a minister say many times that he encourages people who are trying to break bad habits to say to themselves, "I am the righteousness of God," even as they are in the very act of doing the wrong thing. That sounds counterintuitive but what the person is actually doing is repeatedly declaring how God sees them and eventually that change comes to pass. They began to consistently see themselves the way God saw them. God's Word packs a powerful punch—use it so you can **live to win**!

When you believe that His promises are true, and you make a habit of speaking them, you are building upon your knowledge that God loves you. Your increasing knowledge of His very personal, limitless, and no-matter-what love is the basis for everything that you receive from God—acknowledging that He has lovingly provided whatever you need to receive.

Even if you're not experiencing the thing that you desire, even if you can't see it, touch it, taste it, or somehow experience it with your five senses, it does not matter. No matter what you're going through, if God's Word says it, speak it out loud to yourself frequently and then trust it to be true for your life. You'll be speaking Life to your life.

## Live Life Speaking Life

One way to make "speaking life" a habit is by incorporating meditation of God's Word into your regular routine. "Meditation" is defined as contemplation, reflection, rumination, and spiritual introspection (Source: Dictionary.com). Most people relate this word with Transcendental Meditation ™, a "new age" technique based on Hindu writings. But did you know that there is a *biblical* form of mediation?

Joshua 1:8 (NIV) gives great insight into what biblical meditation is and how it differs from TM or any other type of meditation.

> *"Keep this Book of the Law always on your lips; meditate on it day and night, so that you may be careful to do everything written in it. Then you will be prosperous and successful."*

In this verse, God is instructing Joshua about how to succeed as the new leader of Israel after Moses' death. But we can also glean from this scripture about how to be successful in life *today.*

"Meditate" here means to ruminate, to vocalize, to imagine, to speak with oneself (muttering) in a low voice (whisper). It is not simply reading the Word and thinking about it for a brief moment. Biblical meditation involves using your voice to affirm

God's Word for your life and is an action you can take throughout the day.

But God didn't tell Joshua to say anything and everything that came to his mind. He instructed him to meditate on the Book of the Law. God wanted Joshua to read, think about, *and* mutter God's words! He wanted Joshua to ruminate the good things about God and His love for him and the people of Israel.

Rumination usually brings to mind the picture of a cow chewing its cud. When a cow chews its cud, it is regurgitating the food it has eaten earlier, chewing it again, swallowing it, and then regurgitating again, chewing again, and swallowing that same food to gain the most nutritious value out of the food.

We are to do the same in our meditation of God's Word. To gain the most value from God's words of life, read His Word, speak His Word, and think about it repeatedly during our waking hours. Do this so that the Word becomes part of you.

This process of meditation will bring great peace of mind as promised in Isaiah 26:3 NLT:

*You will keep in perfect peace all who trust in you, all whose thoughts are fixed on you!*

Focusing on Him through meditation of Scripture is a way of being dependent on God and He will view that as an expression of trusting Him. E. W. Kenyon, a 19th century pastor, taught that faith talks in the language of God and doubt talks in the language of man. It's always best to confess the ability of God, so that you experience victory and success.

"Let the world hear you confess what God's ability is in you. They have heard your confession of weakness and failure. Now change your song and sing the song of a victor. Everytime you confess weakness, you become weaker. Everytime you tell people about your sickness, you grow worse. Everytime you tell people about your lack, you have more lack. Begin to confess your fullness, the ability of God to make good." ~E. W. Kenyon

www.EvangelineColbert.com

## The Secret Language of Success

There is a secret *language* of success. It is found in Scripture. It is a language that brings life to your circumstances because you are verbalizing the promises of God. Become fluent in God's language of success. Let your vocabulary reflect His desires for your life. Speaking the word of God makes a difference in your situation when it is spoken in faith. It increases your ability to change the direction of your life. Jesus spoke the language of success and so should we. He gives us three examples of how he did it in Matthew, chapter 4.

Let me set the scene:

> After getting baptized along the shores of the Jordan River by John the Baptist, Jesus received the baptism by the Holy Spirit. As a human being, He was now infused with the power of the Holy Spirit. Jesus then went without food for forty days while living alone in a wilderness area. Imagine how hungry, lonely, and exhausted He would have been without the power that had been imbued upon Him by the Holy Spirit before leaving the Jordan River.

> That anointing of the Spirit enabled Jesus to endure not only hunger and exhaustion but also the temptations, taunting, and torment from the devil. It is recorded that *at least* three times, the devil attempted to deceive Jesus so that He would doubt God's love, feel all alone, and look upon Satan as His only provider of good things in the world. Lies, all lies!

Notice that Jesus did not remain silent when the devil began to taunt Him and speak lies to Him. He responded to *every* attempt to get Him to doubt His Father's love and Lordship. Each time, His response was "It is written…" He was referring to or quoting the words God the Father had spoken, as recorded in the Scriptures.

Jesus was clearly showing us two things—that we should respond to *every* lie that Satan throws our way *and* that our response to our enemy's taunts should *always* be based on the words God has spoken in Scripture. Why? Because the answer to every problem we experience can be found in His words. The Word is the seed of what brings us victory. It is alive, powerful, energizing, able to cut through to the heart of the matter, and it always bears good fruit.

Authority can be found in the Word. We use that authority by speaking it. Declare it in Jesus' name in the midst of any problem you face. Jesus has given you the authority to use His name (Luke 10:38). His name is potent. It breaks the power of the devil and empowers you to reign in life. But you must choose to use it.

Yes, this will take some effort. But you want to **live to win**, right? It will require setting up a routine based on God's promises. Here is a very easy way to establish an effective routine:

> Search the scriptures to discover the valuable nuggets of Truth that apply to your situation. (Use a concordance to search for words that relate to your issue.)

> Write those truths and promises down on paper. Writing is proven to be a means of enhancing the process of getting the information embedded in your mind and heart.

> Hear yourself speak those words as you craft your prayer around them.

> Hold tightly to those truths by letting them become your daily affirmations so that your belief in them will remain strong.

It's work but the payoff will be life, healing, prosperity, and good success. You'll **live to win**!

Jesus tells us more about that secret *language* of success in Matthew 4:4. He does so by **quoting a scripture**, Deuteronomy 8:3—"It is written, man shall not live by bread alone but *by every word that proceeds from the mouth of God.*" In other words, it takes more than sustenance for the body to really live.

The word "live" in that passage has a very rich meaning. In the Greek, the word is "zao" which means to enjoy real life, to be fresh, strong, efficient, and having living, vital power within.

Essentially, Jesus said, that in order to **live to win**, you must live by the words that have come from God's mouth!

The winning *modus operandi* used by Jesus Himself was to speak the words of God to His troubling circumstances. By doing so, He made the enemy leave. Speaking the Word also resulted in Jesus being ministered to by angels. This is right in line with Scripture:

*Are they not all ministering spirits, sent out to render service for the sake of those who inherit salvation?* Hebrews 1:14 NASB

*Bless the LORD, O you his angels, you mighty ones who do His word, hearkening to the voice of His word!*
Psalm 103:20 RSV

"Harkening," means listening for and acting upon what's heard. Today, those angels are still available to work; when they hear someone speak God's words, they act upon them. Mankind is the vessel that must speak the Word to initiate action from God's angels. Even in what appeared to be dire straits, Jesus didn't fall for the deception of His enemy.

This was not because He was some super-human. It was because He was human with the supernatural presence of God residing inside of Him. We have that same capability—the Spirit of God Himself resides in us when we make Jesus our Savior. Therefore, we can speak God's words like Jesus did and be assured of the same results—the devil will turn tail and leave.

*The Spirit is the One who gives life. The flesh doesn't help at all.*
*The words that I have spoken to you are spirit and are life.*
John 6:63 HCSB

## Power Infusion Time = P.I.T. Stop

It's important to find ways to infuse the power of God into your life. Psalm 1:3 NLT shows us that the people who frequently meditate on God's Word *"are like trees planted along the riverbank, bearing fruit each season. Their leaves never wither, and they prosper in all they do."* If you were to meditate on that particular verse, you could frequently whisper to yourself throughout the day, "I am like a tree planted near water, always bearing fruit at the right time, never shriveling or unhealthy, always prospering."

Change the words if you like, but think *and speak* about how God loves you and firmly establishes you for success through His Word in *every* area of your life. There's something in the Word of God that is the solution for our every problem and need. *Speaking* God's Word is one of the keys to unlocking and unleashing its problem-solving power. Make sure to include His words in your daily prayers.

The Bible instructs us to pray without ceasing (1Thessalonians 5:17). On a practical level, that's almost impossible to do considering that we have jobs to go to, family care responsibilities, community activities to attend, and need six to eight hours of restful sleep. But if we take short bursts of time and use them for praying in the Spirit, we can actually pray at the same time we're doing something else. This is the only multi-tasking that I recommend!

You could look at these short bursts of time as the pit stop that racecar drivers make during their hours-long race. They pull over and stop...they stop not only to get tires changed, but to refuel their bodies and the car. What if we "pulled over" throughout the day to refuel the most important part of us—our spirit? How much better would life be? I think we'd be much more likely to decrease our defeats and increase our victories.

I have found "pulling over" can easily be done in snippets of 60 seconds here and there throughout the day. These P.I.T. stops are the means of praying without ceasing because we can pray in the spirit even while we are physically doing another activity. This prayer does not require the mind to be fully engaged in it because it's our *spirit* that's praying. That's why we can still be involved with another task at the same time that we are praying in the spirit.

The devil can sometimes jam your words when you're praying in your understanding—in your everyday native language. He works to distract you any way he can. You may find your thoughts are wandering. You may wonder if you're praying about the right things or if you're using the right words that appropriately address the issue you're bringing to the Lord.

But the devil doesn't understand the language of praying in the Spirit because it is the Spirit of God who is praying through you. It's as if you're a World War II Code Talker, speaking in a way that the enemy can't decipher. The devil finds it harder to distract you when you're praying this way. When you call on the Holy Spirit to pray through you, He prays the perfect prayer—in a language Satan and his minions don't understand and can't interrupt.

To become more diligent at doing these P.I.T. stops to pray in the Spirit, I set the alarm on my phone to go off at a specific time every day, Sunday-Saturday, to remind me to take just 60 seconds, right at that moment, to meditate on God's Word or to pray in the Spirit. It doesn't matter whether I'm driving, working, at the grocery store, or involved in some other activity, I can quickly pray in the Spirit and know that my prayer carries the wisdom and powerful influence of the Holy Spirit.

I can't tell you the level of peace I've begun to experience and the insights for my life that I've gained just by incorporating this quick habit into my day. It's like answering a call of love from God. It has made a huge difference in how I view God's love for me and His work on my behalf.

Frances J. Roberts, expressed the advantage of taking time to answer God's call of love in her book, *Come Away My Beloved*:

> "Tarry not for an opportunity to have more time to be alone with Me. Take it, though you leave the tasks at hand. Nothing will suffer. Things are of less importance than you think. Our time together is like a garden full of flowers, whereas the time you give to things is as a field full of stubble. You will receive insight that will give you sustaining strength."

These pit stops are a time for infusing power into your life. You'll empower yourself to **live to win** by incorporating a habit of speaking Scripture (or phrases framed on Scripture) throughout your day. P.I.T. stops are an ideal time to dedicate to praying in tongues. Praying in the Spirit *is* praying in tongues:

> *For the person who speaks in another language is not speaking to men but to God, since no one understands him; however, he speaks mysteries in the Spirit.* ... 1 Corinthians 14:2 HCSB

*A person who speaks in tongues is strengthened personally, but one who speaks a word of prophecy strengthens the entire church. ... For if I pray in tongues, my spirit is praying, but I don't understand what I am saying. Well then, what shall I do? I will pray in the spirit, and I will also pray in words I understand. I will sing in the spirit, and I will also sing in words I understand.*
1 Corinthians 14:4,14-15 NLT.

Jesus declared that praying in tongues would be a sign that believers would experience once the Holy Spirit came to dwell inside them (Mark 16:17). But it's not only a sign that the Holy Spirit has brought power into your life. It is also the *means* by which your spiritual battery gets charged. You build yourself up when you pray in tongues.

> *"Speaking in tongues builds you so that you can believe God instead of your circumstances."*
> ~Norvel Hayes

Praying in tongues is a way of making a powerful connection with the only One who can transcend all obstacles and barriers in your life. Developing this habit of prayer will transform your present life into something so much better.

*In the same way the Spirit also joins to help in our weakness, because we do not know what to pray for as we should, but the Spirit Himself intercedes for us with unspoken groanings.*
Romans 8:26 HCSB

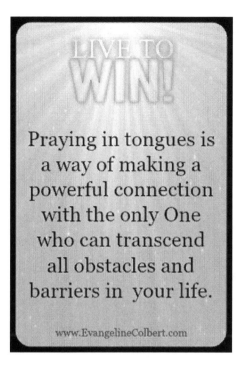

Praying in tongues is a way of making a powerful connection with the only One who can transcend all obstacles and barriers in your life.

www.EvangelineColbert.com

## Declare— "This Blessing is Mine"

When a baseball is hit into the outfield and two players begin running toward it to catch it, one of them starts yelling, "I got it! I got it!" Why is he yelling that? Two reasons—one, he wants the other guy to get out of the way; and secondly I believe he's also confirming within himself, "This ball is mine, I *will* catch this ball."

We can do the same thing with God's promises. We can declare, "This blessing is mine, I *will* receive this blessing." But it's imperative that we audibly speak it; we need to hear ourselves saying it so that we strengthen our belief that it is true.

There are great benefits to speaking God's Word out loud. Don't be afraid to do so even *before* you see the manifestation of your desire. Your declaration is the voice of His Word on the earth and exerts the power of faith. Confess it and let your words only reflect your belief in His. Hold on to what He has spoken. To do otherwise is to doubt His integrity.

Consistently speaking the Word will:

> Cause faith to grow (Romans 10:17)

> Sow seed for what you desire (Mark 4:14)

> Transform your mind to think like God thinks (Romans 12:2)

> Change your attitude about your situation (Ephesians 4:23 NIV)

> Help you to see Jesus in the midst of your situation (Hebrews 12:2)

> Empower you with favor (Ephesians 4:29)

Faith in *anything* comes by repeatedly hearing about it. It doesn't matter if it's positive or negative; the more you hear it, the more you believe it. Joseph Prince has said, "The reason people find it hard to walk in faith is that they are not saying enough of the Word." So make it a point to increase your usage of Scripture by

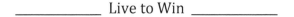 

speaking it aloud. The ears of your spirit perk up when something Word-based is coming out of your own mouth.

## Speak to the Mountain

In Mark 11:23, Jesus said that if *you* would speak with faith to the mountain (of debt, disease, depression, etc.), the mountain would be removed.

> *"For assuredly, I say to you, whoever says **to** this mountain, 'Be removed and be cast into the sea,' and does not doubt in his heart, but believes that those things he says will be done, he will have whatever he says."* Mark 11:23

Ever heard the saying, "You're making a mountain out of a mole hill?" Have you noticed that the more you focus on a problem, the more you will tend to worry about it, and the bigger it *seems* to get?

**What you focus on gets bigger in your life.**

It's hard to look beyond the problem when we're so focused on it. We get near-sighted and anything beyond the problem is fuzzy or completely out of our line of sight. Imagine that someone else is on the other side of the mountain. If you were standing at the base of the mountain, would you see them? No, your view is fully obscured by the mountain. All you would see is the mountain.

It's not until you reach the top of the mountain—when the mountain is "under your feet"—that you can look down on the other side and see clearly who's there.

Imagine again that Jesus is on the other side of your problem but you can't see Him because you're so focused on the problem. It has been magnified simply by your attention to it! He's there, but you don't notice His presence. That's why:

- Psalm 121 tells us to lift up our eyes---to look *beyond* the mountain (problem) and look to God.
- Psalm 97:5 tells us that mountains melt with one look at God. The Word *is* God so when we speak the Word to the mountain (problem), it must respond!
- Ezekiel 6:3 tells us that God Himself *speaks* to mountains.

Since we are made in God's image, we should also speak to the mountainous problem. He wants us in a position where the problem is under our feet. When our focus is on Him, that problem comes under our authority in Christ and no longer hinders us from experiencing the abundant life He longs for us to enjoy. In order to achieve this, He has given us this method— believe and *speak*. This method is so vitally important because it's the method by which we get saved (Romans 10:9,10)!

*Have you ever had a conversation with your problem and told it where it needs to go? Have you ever issued it a cease and desist order?*

You can *choose* to use the creative and life-giving power of your words to have that conversation. With your God-given authority, you can issue the cease and desist order.

The best way to infuse your words with life and authority is to say what the God of the universe has said about the problem. When you speak His words and His promises found in the Bible, you're using His authority to speak **to** the mountain. By doing so, you are putting the mountain under your feet. *When you speak His Word you are removing barriers to abundance and success.*

When you say what God has said, you are connecting to Jesus because He *is* the Word. Release the power of God by speaking the Word of God. Then you can confidently expect that problem to respond to His authority.

What would you say your words in your everyday conversations reflect: abundance or lack, hope or despair, joy or depression, life or death? You determine what you use your mouth to impart into your life—negativity or positivity. Now is the time to make a shift in what and who gets your attention.

Remember, what you focus on grows bigger in your life. Choose to focus on Jesus and watch Him display His power through your words of *life*. Make a shift in focus and look at Jesus' ability, instead of your own, to change things for the better.

- If your mountain is poor health, talk to that mountain like Jesus the Healer is healing you NOW.
- If your mountain is debt, talk to that mountain like Jesus the Provider is providing for you NOW.
- If your mountain is poor family relationships, talk to that mountain like Jesus the Counselor is counseling you NOW.
- If fear is your mountain, talk to that mountain like the God of the universe is loving and protecting you NOW.

Never let the enemy convince you that your mountain is too big. **God is bigger than your mountain.** He's bigger than all your mountains *combined*. Allow His loving power to work on your behalf. Speak the Word to the mountain and expect big things to happen.

Speaking is how anyone increases his or her belief in any "thing." It doesn't matter if the thing is biblical or humanistic, proper or improper, good or evil. Your belief in it is built upon what you've heard about it. Choose to agree with God by speaking His words—speak Life to your life. Your words matter—they are containers of spiritual power. You can't speak defeat and expect victory. Let your words agree with God's words so that you **live to win**.

Say the same thing that He says about your circumstances. Engage in the nature of God—His love, His favor, His plan of success for you—by believing and speaking His words. Allow them to work to change your circumstances.

Declare God's words over your circumstances with boldness and expectation. He's there, living inside you, to perform everything that He said so that you can **live to win** (Jeremiah 1:12).

Speak life— you've been silent far too long!

This next Champion Conditioning exercise will help you consider whether you consistently *speak* to win and how you can speak to win more often.

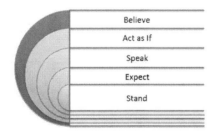

# *CHAMPION CONDITIONING*
## Speak to Win

***AFFIRMATION:*** *I live to win by changing **my** words to align with **God's** words about my circumstances. I choose to speak Life to my life everyday.*

What is the circumstance that seems like a mountain that *you* need to talk to today?

What words of power and promise from Scripture will you say to that mountain today? (Be sure to note the Scripture verses so that you can quickly reference them in the future.)

Schedule a time(s) to make a **daily P.I.T. Stop** to infuse power into your day on a regular basis. You can pray, affirm Scripture, pray in tongues, express gratitude to God—it's up to you to determine your method of power infusion. Remember to set an alarm on your cell phone as a reminder to take this 60-second power break.

### Day and Time(s)

Monday_____

Tuesday_____

Wednesday_____

Thursday_____

Friday_____

Saturday_____

Sunday_____

# LIVE TO WIN!

*Your* words have power. They are shaping what you will experience in the days ahead.

*The tongue has the power of life and death.* Proverbs 18:21 NIV

www.EvangelineColbert.com

# 4

---

# EXPECT TO WIN

*This resurrection life you received from God is not a timid,*
*grave-tending life. It's adventurously expectant, greeting God*
*with a childlike "What's next Papa?"* Romans 8:15 NLT

Maintaining high expectations is a life skill worth learning. Today's top motivational speaker, Les Brown, has said, "If you want to be successful, you've got to *expect to win*. Let that be who you are. Embrace this day with a spirit of positive expectation as you move forward in pursuit of your dreams." When you are expecting good things to happen, you are preparing yourself for blessings.

As you speak God's Word, have confidence in it and expect that His Word will work and come through on your behalf. Hope is having positive, confident expectations that something good *will* happen. Anticipate that His promises will be manifested in your life. It is imperative to have a vital and dynamic hope.

Stay focused on the good that God wants to do in your life, on the good things He has promised. You can live every day expecting to receive good things from Him, looking forward to enjoying what's coming your way and anticipating good results.

> *"High expectations are the key to everything."*
> ~ Sam Walton, founder of Wal-Mart

Focus on Jesus and don't allow fear to diminish your hope. Don't allow fear to decrease your level of expectation and anticipation of good coming to your life. Instead, imagine a new outcome that serves to reverse your fear and puts you on a path that leads to new victories.

The devil would like nothing better than to have you believing that tomorrow is when you'll get your answer from God. The problem with thinking this way is that *tomorrow never comes!* Mark 11:24 encourages us to believe that we have what we desire when we pray. In other words, even if you can't see it right now, believe that it's yours today, not tomorrow.

> *"I tell you, you can pray for anything, and if you believe that you've received it, it will be yours."* Mark 11:24 NLT

## H.O.P.E.

I love acronyms. They help me to remember important things in an easy way. Here's one that I use so that I think about hope in the way it is reflected in the Bible. Hope is not *wishing* for something to happen, all the while not being sure if it will. Biblical hope involves trusting that God *will* come through.

Natural human hope is generally no more than wishing. You never know if what you wish for will come to pass. But when you base your hope on a promise that God has made, you can expect good results.

Hope is:

Having

Only

Positive

Expectations

Hope is a form of expectancy. It is not passive. It is active and always looking for the fulfillment of all of God's promises. The issue of maintaining hope is actually a matter of confidence— having confidence that Jesus is always present and always willing. Be confident that He is wise, reachable, able to help, and willing to act because He loves you like no one else ever will. Because of Jesus' love and grace, we are positioned to live so that we can have only positive, confident expectations of good things coming our way.

Jesus' grace is not some namby-pamby, "well now, isn't that precious" kind of thing. It is the force that saved us and favors us (Romans 8:24). It is the force that empowers us to **live to win**! It is a result of His undying love for us—His "no-matter-what" love.

The best thing about hope is that it is for all time; it is eternal. Like His love, it does not have an expiration date. There will always be more than enough of it to strengthen us through any situation in life and keep us expectant of good things to happen in our lives.

Those good things are a result of His love. As a popular song asks, are you "looking for love in all the wrong places?" Are you expecting what you need to come from people or places other than God? Look only to Him to fulfill your desires and needs. Confidently expect to see the manifestation of God's love very personal love for you in very real and tangible ways.

> *"If you **expect** to lose, you will.*
> *If you **expect** to be average, you will be average.*
> *If you **expect** to feel bad, you probably will.*
> *If you **expect** to feel great, nothing will slow you down."*
> ~Zig Ziglar

## Flowing in His Overflow

Place your hope in God's ability and willingness to provide everything He has promised. When you believe in God as the source of your hope, you'll find yourself being filled with joy and peace. You'll find yourself flowing in the overflow of His abundance. You'll *enjoy* trusting Him because you'll have a confident expectation that He is able to exceed all of your hopes and dreams (Ephesians 3:20).

God has hands (Psalm 92:4) and they are open, not closed, because He is willing to freely give good gifts and perfect gifts to all. He wants to provide us with a constant flow of grace as we make requests of Him. He is the supplier of all our desires. He is willing for us to take from Him as much as we want.

Trust in God is initiated and increases as you stay in the Word and receive comfort from the Scriptures. Joy and peace come as you keep your thoughts on Him throughout the day, enjoying His presence.

## How to Mix Expectancy with Your Faith

Faith in God is required to live a life filled with His love and His blessings. Trusting Him means we believe He exists and that what He says is what will be. The more we focus on Him and believe in what He has said in His Word, the more we change how we think.

But simply believing is not enough. We must mix expectancy with our faith. We must *expect* that God will do what He said He would do. Anticipating that God will come through on our behalf means that we trust what He has promised. And when we trust His integrity about His promises, we can live expecting that His promises will be manifested in our lives.

Psalm 27:13 encourages us to live with expectancy:

*"What would have become of me if I had not believed to see the goodness of the Lord?"*

Pay attention to the key portion of this verse, "believed to see." That's expectation. Notice the order of the words—it's not "see to believe", it's "believe to see." Believing with expectation comes first and then seeing the manifestation comes afterward.

Expectation is a high level of confidence that something will happen, in this case, that the goodness of God will be manifested. Instead of having a fearful attitude about your life's circumstances, maintain an expectant attitude for good things to come from God's hand to yours. It's always helpful to focus on Jesus' love and integrity and not allow fear to diminish your hope.

When you pray, do you *expect* to receive what you've requested from God? Expectancy should be mixed with your faith. Not only are you asking God to do something that He has already promised in His Word, you are also mixing expectancy with your faith in His promises. You do so by looking forward to the fulfillment of the promises and by acting as if that fulfillment has already occurred. Faith says, "I have what I'm believing and asking for. I'm expecting victory!"

I once read a story of a little boy whose town had been experiencing drought conditions for quite some time. He asked his mother if they could pray together and ask God for rain. She did so willingly, excited that her son wanted to communicate with and trust God.

Later that day, as they left home to run errands, the little boy walked out of the house with an umbrella. His mother asked him why he was taking an umbrella when there was not a cloud in the sky. He replied, "Because we asked God for rain." He **expected** God to answer his prayer!

When you pray using God's Word and have faith in His promises, walk away from that time spent with Him expecting Him to do what He promised. Do so even if it means expecting Him to make a way where there *seems* to be no way. The Bible is clear; nothing is impossible *with* God! What good thing will you expect God to do on your behalf today?

## Keep a Hope-Filled Focus

What do you choose to see? What is it that catches your attention and captures your focus? In Jeremiah 1:11-12, God asks, "Jeremiah, what do you see? Jeremiah responds," I see a branch of an almond tree." Then the Lord said, "that's right and it means I am watching and will certainly carry out all my plans and see to it that my word is fulfilled" [paraphrased]. A note in the Amplified Bible about this passage states that the almond branch was an emblem of alertness and activity as it blossoms in late winter.

Easton's Bible Dictionary expands this thought—the almond tree blossoms in the winter—during the cold, harsh, barren season. The flowers appear in the winter, before the leaves appear in the spring! Jeremiah saw this as hope and God told him that he had seen well. When we stay focused on the Word, especially during the barren seasons of life, we live with a hope-filled focus.

*"Uphold me according to Your word, that I may live; and do not let me be ashamed of my hope."*
Psalm 119:116

Hope is what forms the inner image of what you desire. You should see through your mind's eye the things you want to become your reality.

Hope allows your heart and mind to be captured by that inner image of what you desire. What do you fix your hope upon when it comes to getting the desires of your heart? In your mind, do you *see* yourself experiencing that desire? If you do, then you have hope!

Without hope, it's easy to feel completely alone when you're suffering through the disappointments and struggles. You may even sometimes question God with, "Why me?" or, maybe it's, "Why not me?"

When I was going through the struggle of infertility, I had a friend who got pregnant after just one try at it. You'd better believe I was asking God "Why her? Why not me?" I eventually realized that kind of thinking would not change my circumstances. The only thing that could and would change my circumstances was God's Word. It was His promises of fertility that gave me hope. I needed to be saying and praying His promises instead of whining and complaining to Him. I needed to allow my hope to be fixed on God's solution and not on my burdensome circumstances.

> *"Once you choose hope, anything's possible."*
> ~Christopher Reeve

God's power within us has given us everything we need for life. By knowing and standing on His powerful promises, we are partakers or partners in His divine nature (2 Peter 1:3-4). Isn't that great to know? That's a reason to have hope! In other words, when we make it a point to read the Bible, learn His Word, and trust His promises, those promises to us are certain to make our lives successful in every area. Expect God's promises to come to pass; anticipate God's goodness in your life. Get in position, be in the receiving mode; *expect* Him to come through.

Having only positive expectations means you're predicting and relying upon a positive outcome. Even in mathematics, high expectations multiply the probability of the occurrence of the expected event. Most people choose to make decisions that are "good enough." They determine what minimum level of satisfaction will suffice and then choose to live with that. But wouldn't you want to make the *optimal* decision—the one where no other choice will lead to a better outcome?

Romans 5:1-2 says that we should expect God's glory to rise up within us and rejoice in the hope of His glory. When we do that, we won't feel as if we're fighting our battles by ourselves. We won't need to depend on our "self" to win; our optimal choice can be to depend on and rest in the greater power of God that is within us. With God on our side, we're not fighting this battle alone and we can be assured of victory.

Here are some very practical things I've found helpful in achieving *and* maintaining a hope-filled focus:

> End each night with gratitude for one good thing (big or small) that happened during the day. How did it benefit you?

> Become more attuned to your thoughts and words. Are they mostly truth or mostly lies from the enemy? Choose to align your thoughts with God's truth.

> Practice capturing negative thoughts (lies) at their onset and replacing them with positive thoughts (truths from God's Word). Take a stand, be defiant—don't let *any* negative thoughts take up residence and "build a nest" in your mind.

> Take self-care breaks. You could do one of the following or something else that helps you relax:

~Take a quick, brisk walk

~Listen to a few minutes of soft, relaxing music

~Read an inspirational devotion

~Close your eyes and enjoy a few minutes of silence

and deep breathing

~Reflect on God's personal love for you

~Sing a song of praise to lift your spirit

God desires to abundantly supply you with His grace. There is no limit to His dynamic grace! He desires to show Himself strong on your behalf. His grace is sufficient for you to overcome, conquer, and destroy the enemy that wants to see you defeated in life. God wants you to *expect* His grace to work in your favor.

Zig Ziglar expounded on the importance of expectancy. He said, "Even though you were born to win, you must still plan to win and prepare to win. Then and only then can you legitimately expect to win." Many say that the Law of Attraction works on this thesis: we receive what we expect. But expectancy is most powerful when it is founded upon faith in God.

> *"When God's Word is the prevailing influencer of your thoughts and expectations, faith is strengthened and good success is the outcome."* ~ Evangeline Colbert

## How to Expect the Best

Negativity keeps you from expecting the best out of life. It is easy to start and hard to stop. Here are some ways to help you overcome negativity and expect the best:

> Focus on the good.

> Train your mind to be a "Philippians 4:6 Mind".

> Choose to know that God will come through on what He said.

> Quickly banish doubt filled thoughts.

> Affirm again and again the positive thing you expect to happen.

The issue with expectancy is all about confidence. As you hold on to His promises and don't allow doubt or unbelief to dictate to you what you should do, expect that Jesus will always cause you to triumph (2 Corinthians 2:14). He wants you to live expecting to win!

Take some time in this next Champion Conditioning exercise to consider what you will do that will increase your level of confident expectation of good things happening.

# CHAMPION CONDITIONING
## Expect to Win

**AFFIRMATION:** *I live to win expecting God's words and promises to be manifested in my life because I am positioned for God-given victory.*

**ACTIVITY:** To help you maintain a hope-filled focus, print out several copies of the Faith Project Worksheet **on the next page.** Put the extras aside for future use— when you want to specifically address an issue where you need to increase your expectancy that you will win.

Fill out one form according to whatever desire you have that needs more in-depth attention and pressure from God's Word. Keep it in a place where you can easily and frequently reference it so that you maintain a high level of expectancy.

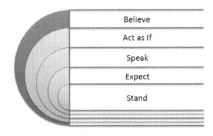

# Live to Win
## Faith Project Worksheet

This activity will help you focus on believing the promises of God, while speaking His Word, and expecting its manifestation.

**Today's Date:**_____

What is the situation in your life that you are addressing with this Faith Project?

What do you believe is God's desire for you in this situation?

List some scriptures that apply to that desire. Set aside time each day to read them.

What will you *say* about God's promises that apply to this situation? Write out your personalized **faith confession and affirmation** using the scriptures above as the framework for your confession.

How often will you speak this affirmation? When? Where?

What actions will you take as a means of plugging into God's promises?

LIVE TO
WIN!

Focus on Jesus and
don't allow fear to
diminish your hope.

www.EvangelineColbert.com

# 5

---

# STAND UNTIL YOU SEE VICTORY

*Don't be afraid. Stand firm and see the Lord's salvation He will provide for you today.*
Exodus 14:13 HCSB

*And he will stand. For the Lord is able to make him stand.*
Romans 14:4b HCSB

While you're waiting to see the manifestation of what you've believed, asked for, acted upon, spoken of, and eagerly expected, there can be additional power added to your season of waiting. You can do more than wait—you can *stand*. To "stand" means that you have a sure-footed confidence in Jesus, His love, and what He accomplished on your behalf. Make a decision to stand in the position gifted to you by Jesus' victory. Trust in Him, His love, and the effectiveness of His finished work on the cross.

Today, I hear many people say that they trust the "universe" to bring good things their way. They speak to the "universe" so that the "universe" will act on their behalf. But if you believe in Jesus as your Savior, you have something better. You have God, the One who is the *creator and sustainer* of the universe, on your side. That means you can speak and stand boldly, knowing that you have open access to the God *of* the universe.

Stay in touch with God. He receives you with open arms every time you come to Him. The Bible tells us that He constantly desires to make sure that your life's path is strewn with every good and perfect gift and that you are *thoroughly* equipped for success (James 1:17; 2 Timothy 3:17).

While you're standing, you will be empowered if you use that time to give Him thanks for the things that He has done. Maintaining an attitude of gratitude is key in making your standing productive as well as restful. When you rest in God, you are essentially saying "Lord, I'm struggling with this problem, **but** I put it in Your hands, because I know You can deal with it, and I can't."

Sometimes it's hard to completely relinquish control of a problem. A lot of us, when we put something into God's hands, will essentially take it out of His hands by worrying. Worry is useless; it does not produce any positive results. Roll your burdens over onto God and trust Him with their outcome (Proverbs 16:3).

Frances J. Roberts helps us see the importance of turning our worries over to God in her book, *Come Away My Beloved*:

> "Never cling to any trouble, hoping to resolve it yourself, but turn it over to Me. In doing so, you will free Me to work it out."

Worry is actually having more faith in what the enemy can do to harm us than in what God can do to protect and prosper us. What is that worry based upon? It is usually based on some form of fear. Even though we may pray about something, we still worry about the issue and look for ways to keep all our options open in case God doesn't come through.

> *If you don't know what you're doing, pray to the Father. He loves to help. You'll get his help, and won't be condescended to when you ask for it. Ask boldly, believingly, without a second thought. People who "worry their prayers" are like wind-whipped waves. Don't think you're going to get anything from the Master that way, adrift at sea, keeping all your options open.* James 1:5-8 MSG

Could it also be that we are afraid that God doesn't love us enough to handle it for us? That's why it's imperative that we renew our mind to the fact that God loves us with His no-matter-what love and He has *already* given us the victory. It's not that we're *going* to win; we've *already* won because of Jesus' finished work on our behalf. So now, we need to *stand* in that place of victory. We don't have to fight for the victory; we need to *enforce* the victory.

You may be wondering how you get to stand in a position of victory over the devil since you're not the one who defeated him. Colossians 2:15 enlightens us: Jesus fought the battle for us and defeated the devil openly on the cross. God set it up so that we get to be a partner with Jesus in that victory.

For example, in our ballpark scenario, you can see the entire team of 25 players enjoy the thrill of the victory at the end of a game even though less than a dozen players actually played in the game. Those few players worked to win the game, yet all the team and all the coaches get to be called victors.

Even the fans and spectators consider themselves as winners even though they never stepped foot on the field. In that same way, we get to enjoy the victory that Jesus won, even though He's the only one that fought the battle and defeated Satan. We did not have to endure the inhumane punishment or shame of the cross but we get to enjoy the victory. Enjoying the victory is part of standing.

Our standing will require persistence; we have to continue to remind ourselves that we *can* stand in Jesus' victory. We have to decide to stay in that position of victory.

There's an old hymn called "Standing on the Promises of God." While preparing this book, I thought about that song, pulled out a hymnbook and looked at all the words of each of the verses. I was shocked to realize that after many years of singing this song in church, I never really paid attention to nor understood what the words of the song convey. Below are the lyrics of this hymn. I've highlighted phrases that really struck me about standing on the promises of God:

*__Standing on the promises of Christ my King,__*
*Through eternal ages __let His praises ring,__*
*Glory in the highest, I will shout and sing,*
*Standing on the promises of God.*

*Chorus:*
*Standing, standing,*
*Standing on the promises of God my Savior;*
*Standing, standing,*
*__I'm standing on the promises of God.__*

*Standing on the __promises that cannot fail,__*
*__When the howling storms of doubt and fear assail,__*
*__By the living Word of God I shall prevail,__*
*Standing on the promises of God.*

*Standing on the promises __I now can see__*
*Perfect, __present__ cleansing in the blood for me;*
*__Standing in the liberty where Christ makes free,__*
*Standing on the promises of God.*

*Standing on the promises of Christ the Lord,*
*__Bound to Him eternally by love's strong cord,__*
*__Overcoming daily with the Spirit's sword,__*
*Standing on the promises of God.*

*__Standing on the promises I cannot fall,__*
*Listening every moment to the Spirit's call,*

***Resting*** *in my Savior as my all in all,*
*Standing on the promises of God.*

*[Lyrics by Russell K. Carter; published 1886; copyright is public domain]*

Here are some important points brought out by the words of this hymn:

> Stand on what *Jesus* said; praise him continually.

> His promises can't fail. When storms of doubt and fear come, the living Word of God is what you say. Say it in order to prevail in a position of victory.

> You are bound eternally to Jesus through His "no-matter-what" kind of love. Remember, God loves you just as He loves Jesus (John 17:23).

> You can overcome daily, using the Spirit's sword— God's Word—effectively employing the promises you find in your Bible (Ephesians 6:10).

> Listen to the Spirit and you won't fail because the Holy Spirit is your life coach and He's giving you perfect advice so you can enjoy good success in every area of your life.

> Rest in Jesus as being all you need; your Healer, Provider, Counselor, Refuge, Friend, ...everything.

Stand in Jesus' victory, trusting in Him. Genuine trust leads to taking a risk and taking action. Just like the first and third base coaches are on the base lines to encourage baseball players to risk moving ahead or to stand still, the Holy Spirit is right there for us as our trustworthy life coach. He's there to encourage us and continue to give us direction as we stand on God's promises. As we rest—confident about His loving help and placing our destiny in His hands—He reassures us that we can always **live to win**.

## Stand with A Victorious Mindset

*"Fight the good fight of faith."* 1 Timothy 6:12

*"Here are my instructions for you. May they help you fight well in the Lord's battles… Cling to your faith in Christ, and keep your conscience clear."*
1 Timothy 1:18-19 NLT

You've got to fight to maintain your faith in God's promises. What are your thoughts like? If someone were to analyze them, would they characterize you as victor or victim? Purpose to have the mindset of a fighter.

A great prizefighter prepares himself mentally as well as physically. He wants to win. He does not let his opponent "get in his head." He does not listen to the lies and taunts of his opponent. How does he accomplish this? Just as he takes a lengthy amount of time to strengthen his body and hone his skill set, he also takes the time to adjust his thoughts long before the fight starts.

He tells himself things like "I'm a winner," "I will go the distance," "I am stronger than my opponent." He recognizes that his thought-life will affect his ability to win. That's why he has other people in his corner telling him those same victory-oriented things.

Think about what you're thinking about. Before you're in the throes of a battle, you too must adjust and renew your thinking. You can purposely choose to think about truth and not lies. You can have a "Philippians 4:6 mind: and choose to think about things that are peaceful and not disturbing, wholesome and egregious.

The Bible says in Romans 12:2, "And be not conformed to this world, but be transformed by the renewing of your min" You "renew your mind" by reading God's Word and meditating on it. This enables you to replace negative thoughts—lies from the enemy— with positive thoughts—truths— that are based on God's promises. Do it as soon as you recognize that you're thinking negatively.

Here's a good example:

Negative thought (Lie): I have been trying to reduce my financial debt for 2 years. I'm so ashamed! It hurts to be around friends who easily afford to do things that I don't have the money to do. I guess I'll always be broke!

*As soon as you recognize this lie rolling around in your mind, replace this thought with a positive one by speaking something from the Word of God...*

Positive thought (Truth): But I choose to remember the Lord gives me power to get wealth, so that I live in the provision of His covenant (Deuteronomy 8:18).

Renewing your mind with God's promises will enable you to stand, blocking doubt and those fearful thoughts. Your mind is the place where your battle takes place. That's why the Bible encourages you to "fight the good fight of faith". It is a fight to maintain your faith.

It is a fight within your mind to maintain faith in God's promises. Affirm His promises regularly to build your confidence that you have the answer to your prayer. But keep this in mind...it's only the truth that you know and apply that will make you free!

Remember that God, who created and sustains the entire universe, is the One who loves you and blesses you. He will enable you to go the distance in this fight against doubt and fear. He will empower you to fight the good fight of faith. Encourage yourself as David did (1 Samuel 30:6). Think about your past victories and answered prayers.

Know that what God has promised cannot be altered. Whatever He has spoken will come to pass because His Word cannot be altered or thwarted (Psalm 89:34). It will accomplish what He planned for you. Rest assured that His plans for you are good and will always give you hope for your future outcome (Jeremiah 29:11).

God never lies nor does He go back on His Word (Numbers 23:19). Therefore, use His unfailing Word and unbroken promises to gain the prizefighter's edge—a victorious mindset—so that you can live to win!

> "Satan's objective is to keep you from obtaining breakthrough in your life. But the prevailing Word of God puts Satan in check and nullifies his every plan."
> ~ Taffi Dollar

## Stand by Praising Him

*"The LORD is my strength, my shield from every danger. I trust in him with all my heart. He helps me, and my heart is filled with joy. I burst out in songs of thanksgiving."*
Psalm 28:7 NLT

Did you know *you* can make the devil shut his lying mouth? You can do so simply by praising God. Psalm 8:2 and Matthew 21:16 confirm that praise silences the enemy. Praise is also a way to strengthen yourself, focus on Jesus, and enable you to ignore Satan's deceitful lies. Each day, take a moment to praise God. Sing a song to Him—it will improve your mood, increase your joy, and generate strength within you.

Tell Him how grateful you are for all He's done, is doing, and will do on your behalf. Let God know that you accept His love for you. Tell Him how you love Him. Acknowledge that he alone is God and that there is no one else like Him. Adore Him simply because of who He is.

Praise is the powerful place in which God dwells (Psalm 22:3) and manifests Himself as being strong. It's in that place where things change because of His presence. So sing a new song to Him. Allow God to put a song in your heart and then sing it back to Him.

Singing praise to Him is like putting on a brand new, fashionable outfit. It puts some pep in your step. It makes you feel lighter inside. It makes you feel better about yourself and life in general. Choose right now to take off that heavy, burdensome garment of shame along with the depressing thoughts that it causes, and put on God's light and airy, joy-giving garment of praise (Isaiah 61:3).

Remember, when you use praise as a tool in your spiritual arsenal, it confuses and silences the enemy. Praise is a form of resistance to the deceitful lies and tricks of the devil. We can build our confidence by using this tool of praise because as we *resist* the enemy, he *will* flee (James 4:7)!

Heaven responds when you choose to praise God instead of reviewing the dreary details of your circumstances. Praise God for His ability *and His willingness* to bring you through to triumph. Mountains move when you speak words of praise, leaning on His dependability. Praise brings peace because it fills up the empty places within you—you're allowing Him to enter into your very being. And instead of focusing on "self" or on your circumstances, He becomes your focus. Praise Him, and then enjoy the peace of God while you wait on God.

*"Your power and goodness, Lord, reach to the highest heavens.*
*You have done such wonderful things.*
*Where is there another God like you?"*
Psalm 71:19

## Stand with an Attitude of Gratitude

> *"Be thankful for what you have; you'll end up having more. If you concentrate on what you don't have,*
> *you never ever have enough."*
> ~ Oprah Winfrey

When someone gives you a gift, do you leave it in their hands or do you take hold of it and pull it toward you? Most of us will grab it and receive it with a big grin on our face and delight in our eyes!

When you take possession of a gift, it becomes yours. You become the owner of it. You can use it however you'd like. You also have the option to put it in a corner or on a shelf and never receive any benefit from being the new owner of it.

Long ago, I realized that the healing of my body was like a gift and I had not taken possession of it. So I purchased a pretty little gold cardboard gift box and set it on my dresser where I'd see it everyday. It was both a visual and tactile reminder that I needed to take possession of what Jesus died for—my *abundant* life. So every time I'd see it or pick it up, I was reminded to say, "Thank you God, I receive my healing."

> *"Oh, give thanks to the LORD, for He is good! For His mercy endures forever."*
> *1 Chronicles 16:34*

Saying "thank you" is an important part of receiving. Not only are you being polite, you're also telling the giver that you're grateful for what they've taken the time to provide or do for you. In my case, I was telling God that I was grateful for His love and for the healing He had already provided for me through the body of Jesus.

I chose to have an attitude of gratitude even when I couldn't see my desired results. I chose to thank God for His goodness, for His dynamic healing power working in me, and for His unconditional love. I started thanking Him in advance.

Thank God for the answer before you see it come to fruition. Thank Him for a good outcome because He promised it, not because you see it. By saying "thank you", you're also telling yourself that you have taken possession of that thing. You are reminding yourself that you have received the gift and taken ownership of it. It also proves that you're trusting God's promise. The promise itself is a reason to be thankful because you know His word is good—you can count on it.

When you hear yourself say "thank you" over and over again with genuineness, you begin to build up your confidence. You're affirming within your mind, through your mouth, that you have what God promised. You're building up your faith in His grace. It is a means of keeping yourself focused on Him and His solution to your problem. You are reinforcing within your mind that you are strengthened and receiving life from Him.

As a believer in Jesus, you are not an outsider to grace—no matter what's going on in your life right now. Remind yourself that Jesus—the Greatest One—lives in you and is on your side. He empowers the believer to stand, trusting in His love. Stand, knowing that you are being empowered by Him to live to win!

## Prepare to Stand

*"If only you would prepare your heart and lift up your hands to him in prayer!"* Job 11:13 NLT

As you prepare to make a stand for what you're believing, asking, and expecting to receive, some "prep work" might be helpful in gaining a firm belief in God's love and promises. Here are seven ways to boost belief and keep you on the path of confidence:

1. Find and repeatedly read scriptures that promise good health until you clearly understand them.
2. Visualize—see yourself in the situation that the scriptures are about.
3. Pray in tongues to edify and strengthen yourself spiritually
4. Speak your affirmation of scriptures that really resonate within you; say them out loud.

5. Speak the Word daily, using "me/I/my" within God's promises that you speak.

6. When you know that you know that you know, ask in faith without wavering. If you're still unsure and have some doubts that what the scriptures promise is really for you, then repeat steps 1-4 until you're not wavering. RESIST giving up!

7. Give thanks daily, taking possession of God's promises through your faith. Have patient expectation of their manifestation, all while remembering that Jesus loves YOU.

Following through on each of these seven confidence-building activities can give you what you need to stand and endure with patience.

In various struggles throughout my life, I've kept a journal, writing down scriptures that applied to my situation. In order to overcome the struggles, finding scriptures on "my issues" and meditating on them became a habit and a priority for me. I knew that in order to live to win in all areas of my life, I would need God's help. His Word contains the solution to any problem I (or you) may face. I would also need the encouragement and wise counsel of friends and family. These were all critical steps of preparation.

Other steps that I took involved writing and audibly speaking scriptures. I chose verses that promised what I needed. Or, the scriptures were in some way related to what I desired. I wrote them in my journal. I wrote them on sticky notes and posted them in strategic places around my home. Now, I also use my cell phone to give me an alarm that acts as a trigger to remind me to read those scriptures and spend time praying in the Spirit. These actions are outlined in Chapter Three, in the section about P.I.T. Stop.

> *Write these commandments that I've given you today on your hearts. Get them inside of you and then get them inside your children. Talk about them wherever you are, sitting at home or walking in the street; talk about them from the time you get up in the morning to when you fall into bed at night. Tie them on your hands and foreheads as a reminder; inscribe them on the doorposts of your homes and on your city gates.*
> Deuteronomy 6:6-9 (MSG)

I hope you'll take the time to find Scripture verses that are applicable to your circumstances. Use them, as God directs you, to pray for the things you desire to receive. Open yourself to how God would have you to pray His Word and believe in the promises contained in His Word.

Dig in your heels—be firm about your faith in His promises. These preparation steps will help you to begin to set the atmosphere in your life as an overcomer. This next Champion Conditioning will help you prepare to stand more firmly.

Stand on His promises and you will **live to win!**

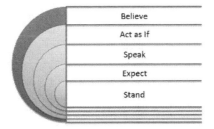

# *CHAMPION CONDITIONING*
## Stand to Win

Here are some suggested activities that can help you focus and stay on your path to victory. Stand and remain steadfast in believing God's promises will manifest in your life. Choose one or two to get started with shifting your mindset from a wavering position to a firm position.

1. Keep a Gratitude Journal. You can do this by writing in a notebook or by speaking it into a memo note on your phone or tablet. Each night at bedtime, record at least one event from that day that you're thankful for.

2. Start new behaviors and routines by using triggers like the P.I.T. Stop and your phone alarm.

3. Incorporate listening to praise music on your ride home from work. It will reduce your stress, shift your focus, and build your resistance to deception. Alternatively, you can write a letter to God or write a poem about His goodness and faithfulness.

4. Refer to your Faith Project Worksheet to speak your daily affirmations. Keep the Worksheet posted in a place where you'll easily see and read it everyday.

5. Do a mindset shift exercise. Replace a negative thought (lie) with a positive one (truth) by speaking a promise of God that affirms you believe you have what He has said about your victory over your circumstances. Repeat as needed.

> **"God never says it's over until *you* win!"**
>
> **~ Jerry Savelle**

LIVE TO
WIN!

Our standing in victory will require persistence. We have to *decide* to stay in that position of victory.

www.EvangelineColbert.com

# *6*

# COVER ALL THE BASES AND HIT A HOME RUN IN LIFE!

In order to hit a home run, a baseball player must touch *all* of the bases before reaching his final destination—home plate. You can hit a home run in life as you purposefully address each of the B.A.S.E.S. covered in pages of this book.

This is a summary chapter, provided to be a quick read when you need to remind yourself of the five essentials for your victory and success. Read the Victory Verses; they will help strengthen you to live like the champion God created you to be.

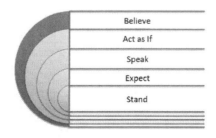

**Live to win,** incorporating these principles in your daily life:

**Believe** that God loves you. Believe that He values you for who you are, not for what you do. Keep a tight grip on those beliefs. Each day, remind yourself of His love. Believe that Jesus has *already* put you in a position of victory. Break the cycle of doubt and defeat. Refuse to get ensnared by doubt regardless of what you see, feel, or experience. Make God's Word the final authority in your circumstances, allowing Him to have the last word about the matter.

**Victory Verses**—Mark 9:23; John 17: 23; 1 John 4:17; 1 John 5:14,15

**Ask and act as if** you *already* have the victory in your situation, even though you may not see it or feel like it. Ask God, using the authority of Jesus' name. Ask for the manifestation of what Jesus died to give you and then act as if it's yours. Use your ability to believe and take action.

**Victory Verses**—Matthew 7:7; Ephesians 1:17-21;Ephesians 2:6

**Speak** the promises of God to yourself daily. Treasure His words. Meditate on His Scripture, keeping your mind focused on His promises. David said, "I have believed, therefore I have spoken." Your tongue can be an instrument of healing because of the words you speak. Deliberately craft your everyday conversations using words that are in agreement with God's promises. Let your words be full of faith and life. Fill your mouth with praise so that you silence the enemy. Allow your life to be touched and powerfully transformed by verbally affirming His Word.

**Victory Verses**—Romans 10:10; Mark 11:23

**Expect** the manifestation of God's promises, because He said so. Keep your eyes focused on Jesus. Expect God's promises to come to pass, because He is a promise-keeper. Anticipate that you'll see God's goodness demonstrated in every area of your life.

**Victory Verses**—2 Corinthians 1:20; 2 Peter 1:4; Psalm 27:13

**Stand** on His promises with an attitude of gratitude and with praise even before you see your desire manifested. Choose to place your trust in Him and not your circumstances. Focus on the Word. Affirm to yourself that you have what you asked for. Let your thoughts be influenced by God's promises, not your problems.

**Victory Verses**—Psalm 71:14; Psalm 100:4; Mark 11:24

When you consistently integrate these 5 key principles into your life, you'll experience increased rest and peace of mind. You will live life with victory and rise above adversity. You'll live life with purpose, effortlessly experiencing the favor of God as you walk in the path He designed for you. You'll live life with a hope-filled focus, being confident that God will do what He said He would do. You'll be able to let go and enjoy the flow of a life filled with God's love and favor.

You'll **live to win**!

LIVE TO
WIN!

It's imperative that we
renew our mind
to the fact that God
loves us with a
no-matter-what love
and He has *already*
given us the victory.

www.EvangelineColbert.com

# *Thank you for reading!*

Dear Reader,

I hope you enjoyed reading *Live to Win*.

When I wrote my first book, *A Seed of Hope: God's Promises of Fertility*, so many of my readers shared feedback with me, insisting that the principles it contained about overcoming infertility could be applied to *any* of life's struggles. Their encouragement prompted me to write this book.

I would really appreciate your feedback. Please let me know what you liked about the book and even what didn't go over so well with you. You can contact me at Evangeline@EvangelineColbert.com. I hope you'll also visit my internet residence, www.EvangelineColbert.com.

Finally, I need you to do me a favor—would you please leave a review on Amazon about *Live to Win*? Here's the link to my Author Page where you can find all my hope-filled books and leave your comments: www.BooksByEvangeline.com. I would really appreciate your input.

Thanks for reading *Live to Win*. I hope the five essential principles I shared have inspired you to make the necessary shifts in your life so that *you* can **live to win**!

I am cheering you on!

Live to Win

# About The Author

Evangeline Brown Colbert is a speaker, author, and Hope Coach. She loves seeing people's lives transformed! She teaches her audiences how to use the power of their words and the Word of God to change their circumstances and to live life victoriously. Her devotional about overcoming infertility is, *A Seed of Hope: God's Promises of Fertility*. It is written from the perspective of her personal victory over infertility. She is also a featured author for Group Publishing's devotional, *If I Can Do All Things, Why Can't I Find My Car Keys?*

As a speaker, she is recognized as a purveyor of hope, bringing practical application of God's Word for daily living. Evangeline's mission is to point people to Jesus by teaching the principle of "Spoken Faith"—believing, speaking, and expecting the manifestation of God's promises.

147

# Books by Evangeline

*A Seed of Hope: God's Promises of Fertility*

*Infertility Sucks—How to Maintain Hope in Your Marriage During Infertility*

## Connect With Evangeline

**Website and Blog:** www.EvangelineColbert.com

**Twitter:** @evcolbert

**Facebook**: www.facebook.com/hopefilledfocus

**Buy her Hope-Filled books**: www.BooksByEvangeline.com

# APPENDIX

# WINNING WORDS

## Quotes contained in *Live to Win!*

**"Relax every strain, and lay off every burden. Let yourself go in a perfect abandonment of ease and comfort, sure that, since He holds you up, you are perfectly safe. Your part is simply to rest. His part is to sustain you; and He cannot fail."**
**~ Hannah Whitall Smith**

"Sometimes the difficulty is not in believing the Word of God, but the difficulty is getting away from some of the things that will settle in our own hearts and minds as being facts, although they were untrue." ~John G. Lake

**"When I do the believing, God does the achieving."**
**~ Jerry Savelle**

"God's Word *is* His will. If you want to know what God's will is, then look at His Word. He only promises the things that He's willing to do. By not knowing His Word, delays in answers may make us think that God is denying us the answers. But by knowing the Word, delays are simply opportunities to stand on God's Word in faith." ~Tom Brown

**"Unbelief is having a higher regard for yourself. Faith is having a higher regard for God." ~ Joseph Prince**

"When you know God will, then He is willing. If you are in doubt about His willingness, He won't. Be convinced, by discovering His promises in His Word, that He is indeed willing to bring good things into your life." ~Charles Capps

**"Tarry not for an opportunity to have more time to be alone with Me. Take it, though you leave the tasks at hand. Nothing will suffer. Things are of less importance than you think. Our time together is like a garden full of flowers, whereas the time you give to things is as a field full of stubble. You will receive insight that will give you sustaining strength." ~Frances J. Roberts, *Come Away My Beloved***

"Speaking in tongues builds you so that you can believe God instead of your circumstances." ~Norvel Hayes, *Confession Brings Possession*

**"Our words act as seeds and when planted by being spoken into our lives, they will produce a harvest. This applies to both the good and the bad things we speak about our lives. The result can be a harvest of weeds or a harvest of good things in our lives." ~Evangeline Colbert**

"Faith proves to the mind the reality of things that cannot be seen by the bodily eye." ~Matthew Henry, *Matthew Henry's Commentary on the Whole Bible*

"There is no failure in receiving from God when faith does not break down."-Anonymous

"The ultimate achievement is to defeat the enemy without ever coming to battle." ~Sun Tzu, *The Art of War*

"Faith gives reality or substance to things hoped for; it is what enables us to feel and act as if they are real. They exert an influence over us as if we saw them." ~ Albert Barnes, *Barnes' Notes*

"Hearing yourself say something aloud is a powerful tool." ~Valorie Burton, *Start Here, Start Now*

"Let the world hear you confess what God's ability is in you. They have heard your confession of weakness and failure. Now change your song and sing the song of a victor. Every time you confess weakness, you become weaker. Every time you tell people about your sickness, you grow worse. Every time you tell people about your lack, you have more lack. Begin to confess your fullness, the ability of God to make good." ~ E. W. Kenyon, *The New Love*

"High expectations are the key to everything." ~Sam Walton

"If you want to be successful, you've got to *expect to win*. Let that be who you are. Embrace this day with a spirit of positive expectation as you move forward in pursuit of your dreams." ~Les Brown

"If you expect to lose, you will. If you expect to be average, you will be average. If you expect to feel bad, you probably will. If you expect to feel great, nothing will slow you down." ~Zig Ziglar

**"Once you choose hope, anything's possible." ~Christopher Reeve**

"When God's Word is the prevailing influencer of your thoughts and expectations, faith is strengthened and good success is the outcome." ~Evangeline Colbert

**"Never cling to any trouble, hoping to resolve it yourself, but turn it over to Me. In doing so, you will free Me to work it out." ~Frances J. Roberts, *Come Away My Beloved***

"Satan's objective is to keep you from obtaining breakthrough in your life. But the prevailing Word of God puts Satan in check and nullifies his every plan." ~Taffi Dollar

**"Be thankful for what you have; you'll end up having more. If you concentrate on what you don't have, you never ever have enough." ~Oprah Winfrey**

"God never says it's over until *you* win." ~Jerry Savelle

LIVE TO
WIN!

You empower
yourself to live to win
by incorporating a
habit of speaking
Scripture throughout
your day.

www.EvangelineColbert.com

# VICTORY VERSES

## Romans 8:1-39 NLT

**1 So now there is no condemnation for those who belong to Christ Jesus.**

2 And because you belong to him, the power of the life-giving Spirit has freed you from the power of sin that leads to death.

3 The law of Moses was unable to save us because of the weakness of our sinful nature. So God did what the law could not do. He sent his own Son in a body like the bodies we sinners have. And in that body God declared an end to sin's control over us by giving his Son as a sacrifice for our sins.

4 He did this so that the just requirement of the law would be fully satisfied for us, who no longer follow our sinful nature but instead follow the Spirit.

5 Those who are dominated by the sinful nature think about sinful things, but those who are controlled by the Holy Spirit think about things that please the Spirit.

6 So letting your sinful nature control your mind leads to death. But letting the Spirit control your mind leads to life and peace.

7 For the sinful nature is always hostile to God. It never did obey God's laws, and it never will.

8 That's why those who are still under the control of their sinful nature can never please God.

9 But you are not controlled by your sinful nature. You are controlled by the Spirit if you have the Spirit of God living in you. (And remember that those who do not have the Spirit of Christ living in them do not belong to him at all.)

10 And Christ lives within you, so even though your body will die because of sin, the Spirit gives you life because you have been made right with God.

11 The Spirit of God, who raised Jesus from the dead, lives in you. And just as God raised Christ Jesus from the dead, he will give life to your mortal bodies by this same Spirit living within you.

12 Therefore, dear brothers and sisters, you have no obligation to do what your sinful nature urges you to do.

13 For if you live by its dictates, you will die. But if through the power of the Spirit you put to death the deeds of your sinful nature, you will live.

14 For all who are led by the Spirit of God are children of God.

15 So you have not received a spirit that makes you fearful slaves. Instead, you received God's Spirit when he adopted you as his own children. Now we call him, "Abba, Father."

16 For his Spirit joins with our spirit to affirm that we are God's children.

17 And since we are his children, we are his heirs. In fact, together with Christ we are heirs of God's glory. But if we are to share his glory, we must also share his suffering.

18 Yet what we suffer now is nothing compared to the glory he will reveal to us later.

19 For all creation is waiting eagerly for that future day when God will reveal who his children really are.

20 Against its will, all creation was subjected to God's curse. But with eager hope,

21 the creation looks forward to the day when it will join God's children in glorious freedom from death and decay.

22 For we know that all creation has been groaning as in the pains of childbirth right up to the present time.

23 And we believers also groan, even though we have the Holy Spirit within us as a foretaste of future glory, for we long for our bodies to be released from sin and suffering. We, too, wait with eager hope for the day when God will give us our full rights as his adopted children, including the new bodies he has promised us.

24 We were given this hope when we were saved. (If we already have something, we don't need to hope for it.

25 But if we look forward to something we don't yet have, we must wait patiently and confidently.)

26 And the Holy Spirit helps us in our weakness. For example, we don't know what God wants us to pray for. But the Holy Spirit prays for us with groanings that cannot be expressed in words.

27 And the Father who knows all hearts knows what the Spirit is saying, for the Spirit pleads for us believers in harmony with God's own will.

28 And we know that God causes everything to work together for the good of those who love God and are called according to his purpose for them.

29 For God knew his people in advance, and he chose them to become like his Son, so that his Son would be the firstborn among many brothers and sisters.

30 And having chosen them, he called them to come to him. And having called them, he gave them right standing with himself. And having given them right standing, he gave them his glory.

31 What shall we say about such wonderful things as these? If God is for us, who can ever be against us?

32 Since he did not spare even his own Son but gave him up for us all, won't he also give us everything else?

33 Who dares accuse us whom God has chosen for his own? No one--for God himself has given us right standing with himself.

34 Who then will condemn us? No one--for Christ Jesus died for us and was raised to life for us, and he is sitting in the place of honor at God's right hand, pleading for us.

35 Can anything ever separate us from Christ's love? Does it mean he no longer loves us if we have trouble or calamity, or are persecuted, or hungry, or destitute, or in danger, or threatened with death?

36 (As the Scriptures say, "For your sake we are killed every day; we are being slaughtered like sheep.")

**37 No, despite all these things, overwhelming victory is ours through Christ, who loved us.**

38 And I am convinced that nothing can ever separate us from God's love. Neither death nor life, neither angels nor demons, neither our fears for today nor our worries about tomorrow--not even the powers of hell can separate us from God's love.

39 No power in the sky above or in the earth below--indeed, nothing in all creation will ever be able to separate us from the love of God that is revealed in Christ Jesus our Lord.

# REFLECTION NOTES
# FOR MY VICTORY

_____

_____

_____

_____

_____

_____

_____

_____

_____

_____

_____

_____

_____

_____

_____

# REFLECTION NOTES
# FOR MY VICTORY

_____

_____

_____

_____

_____

_____

_____

_____

_____

_____

_____

_____

_____

Made in the USA
Columbia, SC
05 August 2017